To Ken and Janet

a trip worth taking

(possibly) The Best (golf) Vacation Ever

By
James C. Coomer

Publishing

airleaf.com

Golf

It is a game one plays against oneself
By rules a player's own ethics must enforce
Respecting customs from an ancient source
And holding game more dear than claiming pelf.
It is a game that humbles the most proud
Regardless of the skill one may attain
The greater hurt the self-inflicted pain
One cannot balm, beseeching God aloud.
Yet, those who go forth eager for the test
Learn something for themselves they may not know;
That golf is but a metaphor for life.
Where all that is expected is one's best
Through all the hazards nature can bestow
The victory is overcoming strife.

Dedication:

To Jane

Whose love of walking golf courses compliments my
love of playing golf courses.

Preface

Traveling with one's wife can be enjoyable. Traveling with one's wife who is a non-golfer on a golfing vacation can be an adventure. Traveling with a non-golfing wife on a golf vacation to Scotland is an experiment. For the golfer, the needs are simple: golf clubs, golf balls, a change of clothes. For a non-golfing spouse, every potentiality must be anticipated so that appearance and attire is always appropriate. For the golfer, food and accommodations are utilitarian. For the non-golfing wife, where one eats and where one stays determines what one wears. For the golfer, the elements are to be endured. For the non-golfer, they are to be avoided. For the golfer, travel between golf courses should be the shortest possible route. To the non-golfing wife, the route should be the most scenic with serendipitous stops along the way for sightseeing.

(possibly) The Best (golf) Vacation Ever chronicles the planning, preparation, and execution of a golfing holiday to Scotland of a golfer husband and his non-golfing wife. From the Royal Dornoch Golf Club in the north of Scotland to Turnberry on the southern coast, the couple accommodates each other's requirements to maximize their individual aspirations of what a Scottish holiday should entail. Written with humor and a colorful description of Scotland, this book could serve as a guide for others contemplating a similar experiment.

Introduction

I have played golf in Scotland in May, I have played golf in Scotland in August, and I have played golf in Scotland in October. I could not make a distinction among the weather patterns of any season. Spring or Fall (or Summer or Winter) the Scottish golfer, or the golfer in Scotland, must be prepared to stay warm and, as much as possible, stay dry. For the Scots, 'nae wind, nae rain, nae golf' is a reality and weather only determines *how* one plays not *if* one plays.

Early one May morning, at my assigned time, I reported to the first tee at North Berwick Golf Club on the East Coast of Scotland. The fact that Bass Rock, rising several miles off the coast, was visible was encouraging. The rain was falling and the wind, as usual, was whipping in off of the water. I gave some thought to returning to the clubhouse to wait out the rain. Looking about, I noticed two Scottish women on the tee area, appropriately dressed for the weather, preparing to tee off into the gale. I thought, "If they are going to play, I am going to play." I lasted four holes. Although I was wearing a rain suit, I was soon as soggy as a biscuit dipped in a cup of tea. The wind rendered an umbrella useless and each time I took my hands off of my pull trolley to hit a shot, the wind blew the trolley and my golf clubs to the ground. The grips of my clubs were wet, my golf gloves (plural) were soaked, my feet were wet and cold and my enthusiasm for playing this beautiful course had waned. As I began looking for a way to play back toward the clubhouse, I couldn't help but notice that the two women in front of me continued, single purposed, toward the next green. I soon discovered a parallel fairway heading back in the direction of the clubhouse and took it. Before I had played three holes in, the rain had stopped, the sun was out, and the wind, though still brisk, was less formidable. My enthusiasm, however, had been drenched and I decided that what I most needed was a nice cup of tea. It took me a day to dry out. When one plans a golf outing to Scotland, regardless of the time of year, one must come prepared for all kinds of weather. One can experience all kinds of weather during one round of golf.

Early trips to Scotland found me traveling with golfing friends. We had come for the sole purpose of playing golf, often 36 holes a day; often on different courses morning and afternoon. If we saw beautiful vistas from any point other than a golf course, it was a bonus. We had not come to sightsee, although in Scotland it is hard not to, we had come to play golf.

I am always looking for opportunities to return to Scotland. Many of my golfing friends do not like to travel such a long distance. Some, who have been once, do not wish to return; they do not like links golf, they do not like the weather, they do not like the food, they do not like the accommodations, (I never considered that perhaps they do not like traveling with me?). I, however, like all of the above, plus the friendliness and hospitality of the Scots. I am always ready to return. Such was my eagerness, that in the summer of 2003, I succumbed to the heretofore unthinkable; I invited my wife to go with me.

My wife and I have traveled a great deal together. We have driven the length and breadth of England and Wales and have wandered around the Republic of Ireland. We have seen much of Europe by train and by car. We travel well together and share the same interests except, she is not a golfer. She loves the beauty of golf courses and genuinely likes to walk them with me while I play but, I knew, if we were going to Scotland together, we were going to have to see more than golf courses and pubs. I, being the sensitive male that I am, suggested that I just play golf in the mornings, leaving the rest of the day available for travel and sightseeing. My wife, being the practical person that she is, pointed out that since we were planning this trip for October, the days, at that time of the year, would be shorter, thereby curtailing the amount of daylight we would have to visit a number of places that were already on her growing list of things to do and places to see. I could sense that I was going to have to be my usual magnanimous self and compromise. It was decided (I believe that I took part in this conversation) that for a ten-day trip I would play golf five times. I could pick five courses and we would plan our travel itinerary accordingly. Since my wife had never been to Scotland, St. Andrews and Edinburgh were required destinations. Fortunately for me, even if I were to be limited to just those two areas, I would still be able to play some of the loveliest courses in Scotland and I would have a difficult time in just choosing the five I wished to play.

Scotland is populated with small towns and villages. Small hotels and bed and breakfast accommodations are wonderful places in which to stay if one is traveling on one's own, or with two or three companions. With advanced assistance in scheduling tee times and reserving accommodations, this more adventuresome approach to golfing in Scotland allows for a brief glimpse of the country and its people that is not possible in a regimented golf tour.

Planning a trip with a non-golfer, however, particularly if that non-golfer is one's wife, requires considerations that transcend the basic necessities of travel that most male golfers seek; clean sheets, hot water, food (most anything will do), and beer. Wives do not like to share a bathroom with strangers, hence; travel accommodations must include a room, en suite, i.e., private bathroom. In our younger days, my wife and I stayed in inexpensive rooms in small European hotels and guesthouses wherein each room contained a small washbasin but the toilet and shower was down the hall. I knew better than to suggest a trip down memory lane. Jane did not require a three or four-star hotel but I knew she would require a room with, en suite bathroom. We would also have to take our little travel box with various size outlet converters so that Jane would be able to use her hair dryer and curling iron. She has a curling iron that operates with a butane cartridge but, several years ago, we had a cartridge confiscated during a carry-on-bag search at an airport in

Germany. We didn't mind. We appreciated the caution. We have returned to the converters, although most small hotels now have hair dyers available. I don't know about curling irons. Jane may have to rough it for a few days. However, in October, with a hat to keep her ears warm, she may not have to concern herself about her hair too much. In the past, we have stayed in some wonderful bed and breakfast accommodations. Wives need not be concerned about comfort.

I, however, had another concern; luggage. Male golfers don't mind playing in the same clothes for several days, providing they are *reasonably* presentable. The basics are a shower, clean underwear, and tee it up. Golfers have rain suits, turtle neck sweaters, wind vests, warm socks, and water resistant shoes; all of which can be stuffed in a golf bag. Shaving gear and other necessities, including a pair of khaki pants and a blue blazer for formal dining, can be carefully stuffed into the bottom of a small carry-on bag. Jane, however, would be packing for a ten-day trip. Although there was a very high probability that no one in Troon would have seen Jane a week earlier in Inverness, the idea of wearing the same outer clothes in each place was anathema. Since Scotland is the home of golf and the Presbyterian Church, of which we are members in good standing, one has to be sensitive to the ecclesiastical edicts governing appropriate behavior when worshipping at either site. Jane is always prepared for any eventuality. My argument was practical: we must dress warmly. Jane's argument was aesthetic: we must look presentable. I shifted to economics: we will have a small car, not a van. She invoked the Patriot Act: we must not look like ragamuffin American tourists who do not respect the decorum of the host country. I had enough experience to know where this was going to end but I plunged ahead fearlessly: "what about airport security?"

"Pish Tosh," she responded in the manner of Lady Catherine de Bourgh dismissing Miss Elizabeth Bennet for a comment deemed unworthy of further discussion.

I could not readily think of a worthy retort to pish tosh, so I bowed to the inevitable.

Preparation

One, of course, does not drive to Scotland from the United States. A Cunard luxury liner might be an elegant way to travel but, if one is going for ten days, five days over and five days back is not a feasible way to maximize one's time. No time for golf, for example, except for driving golf balls into the ocean from the deck of a ship. I logged on to Expedia.com to ascertain when, and with whom, I could fly to Glasgow. I was offered a host of choices and a wide variety of fares. Continental Airlines looked promising. Since Jane and I expected to spend our first day in Scotland driving to the furthest point in our trip, approximately 200 miles, we wanted to arrive in Glasgow as early as possible so that we could enjoy a leisurely drive through the countryside. For a posted fare of $631.52, for each of us flying economy class, Continental Airlines offered a flight that left Atlanta, Georgia at *10:45am* and arrived in Glasgow, Scotland the next morning at 8:00am. That looked promising. But wait!! Continental also offered a flight that left Atlanta at *12:50pm* and arrived in Glasgow at 8:00am the next morning. Or, a flight that left Atlanta at *1:45pm* and arrived in Glasgow at 8:00am. Or, a flight that left Atlanta at *3:15pm* and arrived in Glasgow at 8:00am. Or, a flight that left Atlanta at *4:45pm* and arrived in Glasgow at 8:00am the next morning. I had my choice of five Continental Airlines flights leaving Atlanta over a six hour period but, by taking any of them, I would arrive in Glasgow at the same hour the next morning. A further examination revealed that *each* flight from Atlanta connected with the *same* flight to Glasgow out of Newark, New Jersey. I could either spend most the day sitting in my home in Atlanta, Georgia or most of the day sitting in the airport in Newark, New Jersey I hated these tough decisions.

Since Atlanta is the home of Delta Airlines, and since we have accumulated some Delta Skymiles, I decided to see what choices Delta offered in getting me from Atlanta to Glasgow. For $1466.93, for each of us flying economy class, Delta offered a flight that would require connections in Amsterdam, Holland and London, England before arriving in Glasgow 15 hours 10 minutes after leaving Atlanta. For $1522.35 each, we could connect in Barcelona, Spain before arriving in Glasgow 16 hours 15 minutes after leaving Atlanta. $1517.19 would take us from Atlanta to Zurich, Switzerland to Glasgow in 14 hours 25 minutes. $2029.58 would allow us to go from Atlanta to Paris, France to Bristol, England to Glasgow in 12 hours 10 minutes. I needed help.

On the back of my Delta Skymiles card is a 1-800 number. I called it. Following the offered menu carefully, I said "three" into the telephone. I was instructed to enter my Delta Skymiles number and my PIN. PIN??? I did not have a clue. I didn't recall ever have a PIN. I found the Delta website on my computer and learned that if I had forgotten my PIN, Delta would provide it. All I had to do was request this service and my PIN number would be mailed to me within 5-7 days. I requested this personal service, and then waited. Eight days later a small envelope arrived in the mail with perforated edges on each side. After carefully folding along the dotted line, I was eventually able to rip the envelope apart and holding the two halves together saw revealed therein my secret number. I returned to the 1-800 number and said aloud "three" as though I were uttering "open Sesame" and heard a voice. "All of our operators are currently engaged. If you will stay on the line, someone will be with you shortly. While you are waiting, here is some information that may be helpful to you. When arriving at the airport…" And finally, "Thank you for calling Delta Skymiles, this is Brenda. How may I help you?"

Brenda, as it turned out was extremely helpful. After explaining to her where I wanted to go, and when, she offered me a number of options. I was pleasantly surprised to learn that there was a Delta flight that had not revealed itself on my computer, directly from Atlanta to Manchester, England with a connecting flight to Glasgow leaving within 90 minutes of our arrival. No connections in Zurich, Paris, or Barcelona. 10 hours 45 minutes. Brenda had more good news. There were seats available, both to Manchester and returning, and we could upgrade to Business Class using our Delta Skymiles. Once again, through foresight and careful planning on my part, I had selected just the right choice from a host of options. My wife was, indeed, fortunate to have such a strategic planner as myself working out the details of her vacation. It is true that Agnes Morton, in Scotland, and Brenda, at Delta Airlines gave assistance but it was I who told them where I wanted to go, and when. I had made the big decisions.

Now that I had determined how we were going to get to Scotland, I must now think about how we were going to get around Scotland once we were there. In Scotland, one hires a car, as opposed to renting one. It amounts to a distinction without a difference. My preference has always been, the smaller the car the better. One reason is because petrol is expensive and another reason is that, in the cities, parking is at a premium. Americans are used to cities with large parking lots, or parking garages. The largest cities in Europe were built before the automobile was invented and have simply accommodated themselves, as best they can, for this ubiquitous vehicle. These cities have wonderful public transportation systems, inter as well as intra rail systems, and bus travel. Scotland, however, has only two major cities, Edinburgh and Glasgow, and although there are some wonderful golf courses in and around both cities, carrying one's golf clubs on the train or bus, then walking to an area golf club is not the most efficient use of one's time when time is limited. A hired car is a necessity for an individualized trip. Most Americans are used to cars with automatic transmissions, however, hiring a car with a standard transmission, which requires knowing how to use the ancient methods of foot clutching and shifting gears, can save one approximately $3.00 per day in rental fees. Not a great deal for a short stay but significant for a stay of two to three weeks.

Being a man of a certain age, I always opt for the standard transmission, both in order to save money and in order to recapture, for a short period of time, the manner in which I first learned to drive. Well, all most. In Great Britain, one drives the car from the right front seat on the left side of the roadway, instead of the more common arrangement of driving from the left front seat on the right side of the roadway. This arrangement is not quite as simple as simply shifting seats and lanes. This is a difference with several distinctions. One distinction, if one is driving with a standard transmission is although the clutch pedal is pushed with the left foot, the pattern for shifting gears is just the opposite than it is when driving from the left. The pattern is still the same, shifting from 1st gear through 4th in the form of an H with 1st being the top left of the H and 4th the lower right of the H. In driving from the right, however, 1st gear is the top right of the H and 4th is the lower left of the H. Reverse is usually to be found through trial and error. So the American driver of a standard transmission car in Great Britain, is driving from the right, staying to left, on narrow roads, through frequent roundabouts, while all the time shifting backwards with the left hand. 'Tis neither for the faint of heart, nor for those used to driving with a cell phone stuck in one ear.

My driving record in Great Britain, so far, has been free from accident but not free from apprehension. The High Streets in many small towns and villages in Britain, Scotland, and Wales are better traveled on foot than by automobile; particularly by foreign drivers.

While driving in Great Britain, I need at least one passenger to guide me around the roundabouts. Americans, who are used to roads intersecting at right angles, can age perceptively when confronted with a traffic circle, with cars entering from the right and attempting to exit on the left into one of the several roads sprouting off of the roundabout. When approaching a roundabout, one sees a sign with the diagram on the traffic circle on it and arrows, above which are printed the number designation of the road, i.e., B142, or the direction of a city or town, i.e., Perth. When driving, I need a navigator to shout, "second spoke," or "third spoke," as I enter the roundabout. I cannot read signs, find my spoke, and drive at the same time, although each is required simultaneously if one is to avoid the indignity of driving round about the roundabout several times in an effort to exit in the direction one wished when approaching one of these strategically placed driving examinations.

One other word of caution is in order. Since I, and most Americans, have, for a number of years now, driven cars with automatic transmissions, it is easy, when driving a standard transmission car, to forget a long forgotten routine of disengaging the clutch before attempting to start the car. At least once a trip, when renting a standard transmission car, I am jerked into realizing my forgetfulness as I automatically turn the ignition key only to discover that the car is in a driving gear. This is particularly upsetting when parked closely behind another vehicle to which you suddenly find the front end of your car affixed by a sudden and unexpected surge forward. I suspect such inattentiveness is why car rental agencies require one to purchase an insurance package at time of rental. I have developed the habit of pulling the hand brake each time I park so that if the car lurches because of an inactive left foot, caused by an inactive right brain, it lurches in place and only damages my self-esteem. In addition, most European cars are built so that lights, radio, windscreen wipers, and turn signals operate directly from the battery. They do not automatically cease to function when the ignition is turned off, as in American cars. I mention this because if one parks one's car for several hours to shop, eat, or wander through a local attraction, one may find upon returning, a car with a dead battery. Although a standard transmission car can be easily jump-started (a phrase and process that has meaning only to drivers of a certain age), it is difficult to find the right words in German, French, or Dutch (particularly) with which to ask, "Will you give me a push?" One can immediately see how just the right words are important when asking such a question. Jane and I have, on two occasions, been successful is getting two or three by-standers to push our car. The best method is to find a pub and reward your newfound friends with a pint of their favorite.

Driving is the way to see Scotland, particularly if one is seeking beautiful scenery and the out of the way golf courses. A good road map is essential. When mapping a route to follow, one needs to know that motorways (Interstate highways in the U.S.) are marked with the letter M., i.e., M8. Roads designated with the letter A, i.e., A9, are often two-lane highways, and roads designated, B roads, are secondary two lane roads. The B roads are the less congested and usually the more scenic. These are the roads that wander through the countryside and through the small villages. Most traffic signs are now universal in their meaning. One must be cautious, however. I remember musing, "I wonder what those flashing yellow lights meant at that pedestrian crossing that I just drove through? Why are those people shouting at me?" In the U.S., pedestrians are targets one attempts to drive back to the sidewalk where they belong. In Scotland, pedestrians have rights. Who would have thought such a thing? When anything is flashing, stopping is a good idea.

'To drive in Scotland, one needs a current driving license and in any vehicle one is driving, one must carry the rental agreement and the insurance documents. When planning a trip, I urge taking a moment to check your driving license. How often does one look, seriously look, at something one carries on them every day and presents, upon demand, for purposes of identification? Not often, to which I can testify.

Several years ago, my wife and I were planning a driving trip through Germany. We were going to wander up the Mosel River then down the Rhine River, staying in guesthouses we happened upon at the end of each day, stopping at vineyards along both rivers to sample the local products, and generally to enjoy the country and the people we encountered. At the Frankfort Airport, I presented myself to the car rental agency through which I had rented a car. An efficient young woman dug out the paper work then asked for my driver's license. I handed it to her. She was copying down the required information then paused and asked, "Do you have another license?'

"No," I replied. "That is the only one."

"This one has expired," she said and handed it back to me.

I stared at the license. My birth date is in May. I was standing in Germany in July attempting to rent a car with a license that had expired two months earlier. Dumm! (stupid), as they say in Frankfort. Fortunately, I was not traveling alone. My wife, standing docile, but attentive to my predicament, smiled smugly, nudged me away from the counter with her razor-like elbow, and presented her valid driver's license to the young woman. A knowing glance passed between them, as though a secret sorority handshake had just been exchanged. I found myself standing docilely, but attentive, as the necessary paperwork was completed.

The young woman behind the counter glanced at me and said, "You know that you cannot drive while you are in Germany."

"I understand," I replied. But I had my fingers crossed.

It is so embarrassing to be obligated to one's own wife. Was it my fault that my driver's license had expired? Was it my fault that her vacation had been nearly ruined? Was it my fault the Germans won't let you drive in their country without a license?

To prevent a potential disaster, both foreign and domestic, please check the validity of all documents that will be necessary to insure a pleasant trip or, indeed, a trip at all. Passports, driving license, credit cards, emergency addresses and telephone numbers, are not things one reviews with any regularity. To insure domestic tranquility, check the expiration dates and correctness of each of these during the preparation stage of the trip. Wives may forgive, but they never forget.

The trip through Germany, by the way, was wonderful; although we did learn early that new wine goes directly from the palate to the head.

With the exception of the summer of 2003, during which we were planning this trip, Great Britain generally and Scotland specifically, has a cooler climate than the United States. Early Octobers in Atlanta, Georgia where we live, generally find temperatures in the 80s during the day and high 50s or low 60s at night. The temperatures in Scotland in October, however, range from the low 60s during the day to the high 40s at night. Appropriate clothing is appropriate. My only question was what I would wear to play golf in Atlanta during December. By answering that one, simple question, I selected my wardrobe. Clothing problem solved. My wife asked different questions like, "Who are we going to meet?" "With whom will we be dining?" "In what kinds of establishments will we be dining?" "What do walkers on golf courses in Scotland wear?" "What should I wear to breakfast in a private guest house?" "What kinds and how many pairs of shoes should I take?" I have learned, over the years, to accept these questions with the same seriousness with which they are asked. I was not always so sensitive but one quickly learns that a woman does not like to arrive at the home of strangers only to discover that she is conspicuously under-dressed. No overtures of acceptance, however genuine, can overcome the total mortification experienced at such a moment. Even the most naïve husband, or companion, can immediately sense that he has contributed, in some unknown way, to a humiliation so complete and so utterly devastating as to render his wife, or companion, devoid of any skin coloring. He then proceeds to compound the agony by prolonging the evening as long as possible so that he can avoid what will obviously be a tearful tongue lashing ending with a vow to "never speak to you again," if dating, or "my mother tried to warn me about this," if married. Husbands, who wish to remain husbands, are quick learners when confronted with questions about appropriate dress for events for which he believes the answers to be obvious.

Jane is not partial to cold weather, i.e., anything below 60 degrees Fahrenheit. Since the weather in October in Scotland hovers around her tolerance level, clothing and, therefore, packing became important considerations. For most golfing trips, I pack the night before I leave. What's to pack? In the summer, underwear, a couple of pairs of Bermuda shorts, a few golf shirts, short socks, toothbrush, shaving gear (optional) all neatly stuffed in a carryall bag. In winter, underwear, a couple of pairs of long pants, a couple of golf shirts, a sweater, long socks, toothbrush, shaving gear (optional) all neatly stuffed in a carryall bag. In winter, a windbreaker serves all outdoor purposes. My friend Glenn and I have played courses from Texas to North Carolina nattily attired in our serviceable golfing clothes with never a glance of approbation from fellow male golfers because our clothes were not ironed. (I confess, Glenn and I were pleased when the Greenbrier Resort sent us a card regarding appropriate clothing, when we booked for a golf outing there. Those West Virginians are sticklers for appropriate clothing.)

Jane, on the other hand, was going to need five to six weeks to plan what clothes were to be taken, when they were to be worn, the order in which they were to be packed, and how they were going to be kept presentable while moving from one guesthouse to another; packing and unpacking at several different locations over a period of ten days. *Since clothes for cooler weather are bulkier than clothes for warmer weather, would one suitcase suffice?* ("Yes," I said.) *Since we were to have dinner with two different couples, should she take two dresses, or wear the same one on both occasions?* ("The same," I suggested.) *If we ended up staying one night at the Turnberry Resort, would this same outfit be appropriate for dinner there. After all, it would already have been worn twice in Scotland albeit, one hundred miles apart.* ("Yes," I said, although here I was on unsure footing.) *Would we be attending church on Sunday?* ("No," I replied. "We would be worshiping at a more open venue on Sunday morning, though my participation would be no less devout.") *What if it rains? Should I pack my London*

Fog raincoat or carry it with me onto the airplane. ("Carry it.") *What if it rains while we are on the golf course? I won't be wearing a London Fog while hiking around searching for golf balls?* (Jane's usual endeavor when accompanying me on golf courses.) ("Umbrella," I suggested without catching her eye.) *What about traveling in the car? Won't we be stopping to visit castles and churches, and pubs?* ("What do you usually wear when traveling in the car?" I asked.) *I mean, are we going to stop anywhere where slacks, turtleneck, pullover sweater, and comfortable walking shoes are inappropriate?* ("Since I don't believe the Queen will be at Balmoral when we pass through, I think your comfortable clothes will be appropriate," I ventured to suggest.) *Since we have been upgraded to Business Class, should I wear something nicer than usual?* ("Have you forgotten your style-police comments the last time we were in Business Class?") *Will I have time to change my clothes at the Glasgow airport before we get the car?* ("No. We will have to get on the road immediately if we are going to stop for sightseeing along the way." Then, in an inspired moment, I added, "And anyway, you will look wonderful in anything you will be wearing.") Jane tried not to, but I saw the smile. I was winning.

In the end, we managed two large bags apiece, two small carry-on bags, and the large, protective travel bag for my golf clubs. This travel bag is large enough to serve as an additional piece of luggage in which carry golf shoes, rain suits, wind vests, a couple of warm pullovers, and a dozen new golf balls. Since we would be checking the large bags in Atlanta, we would not have to concern ourselves with them until we arrived in Glasgow. I have never understood why people, who sit on a transcontinental flight for 8-12 hours, do not wish to take fifteen minutes to retrieve checked luggage when arriving at their destination It is particularly puzzling if they have to change flights in the process, requiring them to lug their luggage from arrival gate to departing gate that frequently, for international flights, is in another terminal.

I wanted Jane to see as much of Scotland as is possible on one trip. Since Royal Dornich Golf Club in northern Scotland is both scenic and one of my favorite courses to play, I decided that we would begin our vacation there. This would mean that immediately upon our arrival in Glasgow we would begin to drive to the furthest northern point of our visit, the village of Tain, after which we would gradually work our way back toward the southern part of the country so that we would be near the Glasgow airport ten days later. I had an idea of the route I wished to drive, along the lochs toward Inverness. Seeking guidance, however, I called our friend Jennifer in Houston, Texas. We have never known Jennifer outside of Houston but we know she was born in Scotland and returns as often as she can to visit family and friends. I told her the route I wanted to drive from Glasgow to Inverness.

"No, no, no, no," she said. "Let me tell you how to go to see some things that Jane will love. Do you have your map handy?"

I spread my large Scotland Touring Map on the floor, got down on my knees with the phone to one ear and a pencil in hand. I could hear Jennifer preparing herself similarly 800 miles away. For the next thirty minutes, she outlined a driving trip for us on secondary roads through town with names like Aberfoyle, Lochearnhead, Pitlochry, Tomintoul, and Grantown-on-Spey. We would travel through Balmoral but there was no need to stop there, she said. There was, however, a small Presbyterian Church nearby that we should visit. When she pronounced the names of the towns and villages, another voice came over the line, one that I seldom had had an opportunity to hear. It was a voice from Scotland, modified by the years abroad but suddenly natural, as multilingual speakers are natural as they move back and forth between languages unaware that they are doing so. The rolled r's and throaty consonants flowed through the air, as they must have done when she was a wee lass in the Highlands of the clan, McClean.

Although the distance of our first day's drive was only 200 miles, easy enough to do in four hours on major roadways, I was planning on six or seven hours to wander through the center of Scotland.

The object of any trip to Europe is to stay up as late as possible on the first day because, with a five or six hour time difference, one's body is going to wake up about 2:00am or 3:00am no matter what time one goes to bed. Once on a trip to Berlin, my wife and I found it impossible to stay active past 10:00pm Berlin time; even though we knew it was only 4:00pm body time. I discovered a music station on our hotel room radio and, although it was barely dark, we soon fell asleep. At sometime during the night, I awoke and noticed that the radio was still playing music. I sleepily reached over and turned the radio off. The music continued to play. I hit the snooze button. The radio continued to play music. I turned all of the dials. The radio continued to play music. I began to mutter and awakened my wife.

"What is wrong with you?" she snapped.

"Can't turn this radio off," I responded in exasperation.

"Leave it on and go to sleep."

By this time I was sitting up in the bed shaking the radio, which continued to purr music.

"Damn German technology," I muttered.

I reached down and pulled the plug from the wall. *The music continued to play.* I was by this time awake, irritated, and confused. I walked to the window, leaned on the windowsill, and stared out into the dark. I heard music. I glanced down toward the street and, three floors below me, at an outdoor café, two young men were singing Simon and Garfunkel songs. At this moment, it occurred to my now awake wife that the source of the music was outside the room not inside. She was at this time insufficiently amused by the situation to see humor, since it was clear to her that we had been asleep approximately one hour and we were not likely to go back to sleep for some time. I tried to be contrite.

There is, unfortunately, a coda to this story. We spent the next day in Berlin sightseeing. We had previously been in this city when it had been a walled island. We were excited to see this new, united city. By the end of the day, we had almost forgotten *Eine Kleine Nachtmusik.* Jane, a wine drinker in the U.S., always becomes a beer drinker in Germany. We ended our second day in Berlin at Loretta's Beer Garden, a large, outdoor beer garden, complete with Ferris wheel, several blocks off of the Kurfurstendamm. About 11:00pm, we headed toward our hotel. Seeing a small group waiting for the elevator in the lobby, and knowing how small European elevators are, we decided to walk up the three flights of stairs to the floor on which our room was located. As we approached the door to the third floor of the hotel, we became aware of a piercing noise, loud voices, and the sound of someone banging on a door. As we walked into the corridor, we noticed several people standing outside a door and as we walked closer we noticed that the door outside of which they were standing was the door to our room. The piercing noise we had heard while climbing the stairs was coming from our room. An elderly woman in a dressing gown was banging on our door and my primary German was enough for me to understand that she was not happy. I hurriedly opened the door and discovered that the sound was coming from the radio. During my futile experimenting the night before, I had undoubtedly turned on the wake-up alarm and, when I re-pluggged the radio during the morning, was not aware of it. In fiddling with the dials the night before, I had obviously turned the volume to its highest setting. How long it had been sounding, I did not know but by the time we arrived the other guests had attracted the attention of the hotel's night manager to whom I found myself attempting to explain what had happened. He was not amused. The guests on my floor were not amused. But, for some strange reason, my wife was amused. No, amused is not descriptive enough. She was absolutely reveling in my embarrassment.

For the second night in a row, my wife did not sleep well. The second night, however, was not because she was irritated. It was because she could not, or would not, exercise a little self-constraint to keep herself from laughing. I was not amused.

I was confident that there would be no similar incident during out first night in Scotland. The Golf View Guest House in Tain, where we would be staying for two nights, is at the edge of the town. The area is quiet and rooms are large and comfortable. And, we expected to arrive exhausted and ready for a good nights sleep. We would have no need for an alarm clock. Our hosts would call us up early in the morning so that we could enjoy a full Scottish breakfast before setting out on the day's activities.

Three weeks before the trip, all of the preparatory tasks had been completed. Driving licenses and passports had been triple checked to insure their validity, clothes had been selected, gifts had been purchased, necessities, like a dozen golf balls and several golf gloves, were added, travelers checks secured and currency exchanged. We were ready, and waiting.

Or, so I thought. At about this time our thirty something year old daughter and her thirty something year old husband informed us that we were to become grandparents. My daughter had been pretty sure of her condition for several weeks. This day, however, it became official based on a visit to her doctor. My daughter, explaining to me how it was she suspected that she was with child, enhanced my education in these matters considerably. She had evidently been peeing on some little stick and then watching to see if the stick changed colors. If it did, and if the color became increasingly distinguished, that, in some mysterious way known only to women and their gynecologists, was evidence that the pee-er was, in all likelihood, pregnant. My thoughts flashed to all of the little sticks at the edge of numerous golf courses onto which I had relieved myself. There was something magic going on here that I could not fathom.

Jane and I were delighted at this news. I did a quick arithmetic computation in my head, factoring in the number of weeks my daughter was pregnant and subtracting this figure from the normal gestation period of human females. Even accounting for a statistical error of a week, either way, I calculated the happy event would not interfere with our trip to Scotland.

Jane, on the other hand, was suddenly seized with maternal concerns that transcended time and space. How, she wondered, could she be gone for ten days at a time like this? The first three months of a pregnancy are the most uncomfortable. Shouldn't she be here in case our daughter needed her? She, Jane, had some experience in these matters (once, I pointed out thirty something years ago when the earth was flat) and should be available for comfort and advice. How could she enjoy Scotland if she was worried about our daughter?

I was confused. Not for the first time, I confess, in thirty something years of marriage. Our trip was to take place in October. The blessed event was projected to take place the following April. A piece of this jigsaw puzzle was lost to me. I thought that I had the whole picture but, evidently, I was missing an important piece without which the puzzle could not be completed.

"Jane."

"Yes."

"Let me see if I understand this. Our daughter is approximately four weeks pregnant. Is that correct?"

"Yes."

"Most pregnancies last for nine months. Right?"

"Is this a game?"

"No. I am laying the foundation for a dialectic argument."

"I am sure there will be an important point to this."

"Yes. The point is, if our daughter is expecting to be delivered of a child next April, how does this affect our trip three weeks from now?"

"Are you singularly obtuse?"

I had to think about that.

"What if I am traipsing around some castle or golf course in Scotland and my daughter needs me?"

"What is she likely to need?"

"How should I know until she needs it?"

"Well, she has a mother-in-law and two sisters-in-law who live near. The mother-in-law has had four children and the sisters-in-law two each, couldn't she call one of them while we are gone?"

Why did I feel as though I had just said something that Bartlett could include under the heading, dumbest utterances ever by a husband of long standing?

My wife just looked at me, with sympathy one usually associates with the reaction to the statement, "your dog just got hit by a car." She seemed to resist the temptation to pat me on the head.

"Let me talk with Alice."

I knew in that moment that the persuasiveness of my dialectical argument had been irrefutable. I smelled sea air. I saw heather and pot bunkers. I had successfully weathered another crisis.

Day One

I live on the northeast side of the Atlanta, Georgia metropolitan area. Hartsfield International Airport is southwest of the Atlanta metropolitan area. Although the driving distance is only thirty-five miles, there is a barrier between where I live and the airport; it is the city of Atlanta. Like all large metropolitan areas, travel in and around the Atlanta area is governed by the time of day at which one wants to travel. What makes travel in and around Atlanta particularly onerous is a lack of travel options. Three major inter-state highway systems intersect in downtown Atlanta. Two of them merge at the northern edge of the city, spilling ten lanes of traffic into five lanes and merging two HOV lanes into one. This engineering nightmare bisects the central business district of Atlanta, whereupon it intersects with a third inter-state highway. Appropriately, at this intersection where thousands of tense and irate drivers attempt to navigate themselves and their families successfully through Atlanta, stands Grady Hospital with its nationally renowned emergency room and trauma center. This convenience is purely coincidental.

Atlanta is also blessed with a perimeter highway. Since, by law, the behemoth 18-wheel trucks that carry the nations goods in their bellies cannot travel inside the perimeter unless delivering the goods, the perimeter highway around Atlanta has become the training ground for those drivers wishing to compete in the oval-track 18-wheeler racing circuit. The competitive goal seems to be, which truck driver can get around Atlanta the fastest. Neither rain, sleet, speed limit, nor drivers of smaller vehicles impede this daily competition. At least once a day, someone fails in this objective causing thousands of fellow travelers, depending on the time of day, to stop what they were doing, pull out the cell phones, and pray the coffee that they have been drinking for the past hour does not flow directly through their system in the shortest possible time.

Atlanta also can boast of MARTA, the Metropolitan Area Rapid Transit Authority. Metropolitan is, of course, a misnomer, since the suburban counties surrounding Atlanta have refused to allow this rapid transit system to expand into their neighborhoods. The results of this parochial shortsightedness mean that Atlanta commuters have longer commuting times than any other city in the country. Another major problem with MARTA, something that rapid transit riders in other cities may find incongruous, is that MARTA essentially has only two lines; one north to south, the other east to west. Riders wishing to travel in oblique directions must rely on their automobiles; hence traffic in all directions.

The reason that I am thinking about Atlanta transportation options on the first day of our trip is simple: how are Jane and I going to get to the airport? Our plane departs Atlanta at 8:20pm. Thanks to Osama bin Laden, al-Qaeda, the Saudis, Saddam Hussein, George Bush, and Tom Ridge, we must be at the airport by 6:00pm. In order to meet that schedule, since we live thirty-five miles from the airport, we should leave our house no later that 5:00pm. If, however, we left our house at 5:00pm, we would arrive at the airport at 7:00pm, assuming there were no rush hour traffic delays. MARTA is usually our transportation method of choice to the airport. We can easily get to the northern most station and take the MARTA directly into the airport. On this trip, however, we will be pulling two large bags *plus* my large rolling golf travel bag, *plus* a carry-on bag containing books, maps, and enough cosmetics to service every woman on the airplane, *plus* London Fog all-weather coats, and my tweed hat. I confess, this hat usually sits on a shelf in my closet, unworn, except for trips to Europe in cold weather. I have a golf cap in my golf bag but, if I am going to be wandering about in Edinburgh, I want to be nattily attired and my tweed hat gives me that 'My Fair Lady' cosmopolitan air. All of these appendages make a trip on MARTA impractical. We could leave at 4:00pm, drive to a satellite parking area and take their shuttle to the airport. This would mean getting to the airport three and a half hours before our flight leaves but it is a practical solution. This also would mean adding about $140 to the cost of the trip for parking fees. The solution we decided upon was to inconvenience our daughter by having her drive us to the airport. Even though she was great with child by this time (twelve weeks), she agreed. However, because of traffic, she wished us to leave at 3:00pm so that she could avoid the potential traffic entanglements a later departure might entail. This would mean that my wife and I would have to spend four hours at the airport before our flight would depart. We simply considered this as overhead; the price one pays for living in the big city.

While driving, our daughter assumed the customary role into which adult children seem to naturally evolve; that of parent.

"Do you have your tickets?"

"Check."

"Do you have your passports?"

"Check."

"Dad, is your driving license valid?"

(Smartass) "Check."

"Will you call when you arrive?"

"No! We are going to be in Scotland, not Scottsdale."

"How will I know where you are?"

"We left an itinerary on the kitchen table. In case of an emergency you will know where we are scheduled to be every night. Some of these places even have telephones."

"No need to develop an attitude. Did you stop the papers and the mail?"

"Check."

"Do you have a camera?"

"Check."

"Are you going to take pictures? Usually you go on a two-week trip and take ten pictures. Why bother to take a camera?"

"We promise to take lots of pictures."

"Did you bring something to read on the flight?"

"Check."

"Remember to drink lots of water. It's easy to dehydrate on long flights. Alcohol dehydrates. Mom, make sure to walk around a little so your legs don't tighten up."

I knew her Masters degree in Health Administration would come back to haunt me.

"Mom, do you have enough warm clothes?"

"Yes. I think so."

"Dad, are you actually going to wear that stupid hat?"

"Alice, have I ever been critical of what you wear?"

Mother and daughter stared at each other then, both stared at me.

"What?" my daughter shrieked.

"When?" I demanded somewhat defensive.

"Well, let me see; grade school, middle school, high school, college..."

I changed the subject. "This hat makes me look like Rex Harrison."

"Who's Rex Harrison?"

A generational gap yawned before me. Any answer would be superfluous.

"There is no need for you to come early to pick us up when we get back," my wife said to our daughter. "You can't come to Customs any more because of security. Besides, our plane may not arrive as scheduled. We will call you from Customs when we get back and by the time we clear and pick up our bags, you should be nearly here."

"I know you are going to have a great time," my daughter said, and then added one more piece of maternal advice. "Be sure you stay warm."

We promised that we would.

"Love you," she sang in that voice we knew and loved.

"Love you, too," we responded almost simultaneously. Then, we were left alone to find our own way to the ticket counter, through security, (I had remembered to wear new socks) to our gate, and, hopefully, onto our flight; almost too much responsibility for two adults to handle without assistance from their children.

There is never a good time to visit the Atlanta airport. It vies with Chicago's O'Hare as the busiest airport in the country. Atlanta's airport boasts of two terminals. The two terminals are, in reality, two sides of the same building, which requires that all passengers, whether checking in through the North Terminal or the South Terminal, converge on the same security area; much like the city's inter-state highway system. Having endured the long ticket check-in line, the passenger must now place himself or herself at the end of a doubly long line to be screened for inappropriate possessions. Like all airline travelers, my wife and I have long since accepted the inconvenience, but the necessity, of this increased security. Since we had hours to linger before our flight, we accepted our fate with alacrity. The only inconvenience was a delay in relaxing with a Starbucks coffee in the International Terminal.

The Delta Airlines check-in line was, as always, serpentine. Since we had used our Delta Skymiles to upgrade our seating to Business Class, I lugged our baggage toward the Business Class check-in counter. Whenever I upgrade my seating, I am always apprehensive. I expect to get to the counter only to be told that Madonna and her entourage appeared unexpectedly and bumped me to the back of the plane. Even though I had seat confirmations in my hand, I always expect something untoward to happen, not the least of which would be to be sent to the end of the serpentine, from whence I would wend my way to the counter where the attendant, after glancing at my ticket, would then refer me to the Business Class check-in counter because my tickets had been upgraded. I am happy to say that my skepticism never manifests itself into a Woody Allen scenario, although on one occasion it came endearingly close. During one check-in, in compliance with a requirement now discarded, the check-in attendant asked: "Has anyone given you anything to carry that you do not know you have?"

I pondered that question for a moment.

"Let me try again," she said. "Are you carrying something that you don't know you have that someone you don't know gave you to carry?"

I pondered that question, also.

She smiled. "How about this, she said. "Are you?"

"No," I responded.

"Great," she said. "Have a great trip."

The Delta attendant, all teeth and efficiency, checked our passports, our tickets, our luggage, and our demeanor to determine if we looked suspicious, in compliance with the John Ashcroft Total Information Awareness System.

"Your plane will begin loading at 7:30pm from Gate 4 in the International Concourse. Have a nice flight."

"Thank you," we said and headed for the security area. As I walked away, I couldn't help but wonder if a camera was recording the manner in which I walked so that a satellite could track my amblings through Scotland. "There he goes," some unknown voice would mutter. "That walk is as distinctive as a finger print. I wonder why he stops and swings his arms so much?"

We queued up to participate in the rite of passage required in order to be admitted into the secure sanctuary of airports. We were familiar with the drill: all carrying on materials on the conveyer belt, pockets emptied of all coins and metal objects, the inevitable sounding of the alarm as we passed over the threshold into the inner sanctum of the airport, the wanding, the patting, we both slipped out of our shoes, the inspection of the camera, of the tape recorder, of the toilet articles and, at last, we were inside. We gathered up our coats, Jane's purse, my carryon bag, my Rex Harrison hat and headed down the escalator to the train that snaked through the bowels of the airport connecting the various departing concourses. The International Concourse is the furthest from the main terminal but a haven of rest for weary travelers who were two hours into their trips but had yet to leave the airport.

"I have to go the men's room," I said.

"Fine," said Jane. "I will get us some coffee."

I wandered off to the appropriate facility. Feeling infinitely more comfortable, I was washing my hands when I head a voice.

"Hi."

I looked around. I didn't see anyone.

"How are you?"

I spotted two feet firmly planted on the floor behind the door in one of the stalls.

"Fine," I responded. After all, the greater Atlanta area has a population of 4 million and, at the airport, one occasionally sees an acquaintance, although I did not exactly see this one.

"What are you doing?" said the voice.

"Heading for Scotland," I replied. "Jane and I are going over for about ten days. I am going to play some golf and we are just going to wander around the countryside for a few day. We are going to spend some time in St. Andrews and in Edinburgh and end up in Troon and Turnberry before heading home. Should be a great..."

"I've got to hang up," the voice said. "Some idiot in here keeps answering every time I say something to you."

I made a hasty exit.

My next mistake was conveying this story to Jane as she was taking a sip of coffee. She spewed the swallow halfway across the concourse as she convulsed into hysterical laughter. Every eye swiveled in our direction. My Jane is not a demonstrative person. The last thing that would ever occur to her would be to call

attention to herself in a public place. She was on this
occasion, however, totally unaware of the world around
her. She gasped for breath. She gurgled. Tears ran
down her face creating little rivers of mascara. People
stared at us. Stared at me. She would pause, gulp in a
breath, look at me, and then collapse once more into an
uncontrollable fit of laughter. It must have taken ten
minutes for her to get enough control of her emotions to
head to the women's room for repairs. She paused once
to look back at me, and then turned quickly away,
shoulders shaking as laughter gave way to giggles.
Aware of glances from all directions, I calmly tried to
drink my coffee. After a while, I saw her walking
toward me from the women's room. When she caught
my eye, she burst out laughing again and quickly
retreated back into the sanctuary from whence she had
come. When, at last, she returned to her coffee and me
it was some time before she could look at me without
grinning like the Cheshire cat. I was delighted that I
could be the source of such amusement. I knew, on the
instant, that this was a story that was going to be told
and retold at my expense for years to come. I had to
confess: I deserved it.

Flying time from Atlanta, Georgia to Manchester,
England is approximately seven and one-half hours.
Jane had armed herself with the 870-page *Harry Potter
and the Order of the Phoenix* and I was equally
prepared with the 1040 page *The Years of Lyndon
Johnson Master of the Senate*. Both were hardback
editions and for the next two weeks, whenever we
packed, I had to lug that weight around. Future flights

would find me carrying a Robert Parker paperback; even if I had read it before. We left Atlanta on time at 8:40pm. By 10:30pm, we had eaten, had drunk some wine, reclined our seats and were fast asleep. Day one of our holiday was complete.

Day Two

Somewhere over the Atlantic Ocean, day two began while it was still day one in Atlanta. Our cabin crew, under the ever attentive Priscilla, served us hot towels, hot coffee, and, for us, a cold breakfast; cereal and milk. It was a morning that frequent flyers often experience. The view from the window revealed blue sky and cotton-ball clouds as far as the eye could see. It was as though we were looking down on an Arctic landscape on a sunny day. Nothing but various shades of white met our eyes. Such a scene always makes me feel as though I could bounce along from cloud to cloud. Perhaps in another lifetime, I shall. As we began our decent into Manchester through the clouds, the white transformed itself into a solid gray. Raindrops began to streak the window and as we gradually moved through the clouds, the first glimpses of the English countryside began to appear intermittently. Suddenly the land was there below us. Jane and I have always loved the systematic organization of the English countryside. One recognizes it from the ground but, from the air, the divisions by roads and stone fences present the countryside as though intentionally divided into geometric patterns of squares, parallelograms, and trapezoids. The absence of large groves of trees allows for an unobstructed vista of green fields, both from the ground and the air. Great Britain is a beautiful country.

Our flight from Atlanta to Manchester was thirty minutes early and our flight from Manchester to Glasgow, we were to learn, was to be thirty minutes late. Since we were connecting from an international flight, we did not follow the throngs to the Immigration center but were directed to an area for connecting flights. An attentive young woman escorted us from the terminal to a waiting bus, which drove us to another terminal where we presented out tickets to a man sitting inside a circular counter. Since we seemed to be the only passengers making this particular connection, he called the Customs officials who responded that they would send someone over to check our passports. Ten minutes later a young woman appeared, asked the pertinent questions, stamped our passports, welcomed us to Manchester, and directed us to the area from which our British Midlands Airlines flight would transport us to Glasgow. First things first, however. Where was the nearest Starbucks Coffee?

Jane and I love international airports. The people of the world pass in front of us and we never cease to marvel at the differences and the sameness. While we sipped our coffee, a middle-eastern man seated at the next table was pecking away at his laptop computer. At an adjacent table, three Englishmen in well-tailored wool suits were each chatting into cell phones with brief cases open before them. Eastern Europeans were congregated in the smoking area. With two hours before us until our flight, we simply sat and watched other citizens of the world go about their business for that day. We had enough experience to know that the same scene was simultaneously taking place in airports around the world.

The British Midlands Airways flight from Manchester to Glasgow was approximately fifty minutes. In a little over twelve hours, we had traveled 6,000 miles.

We collected our bags and I called the Arnold Clark automobile dealership from which we were hiring our car. A courtesy van picked us up and as we left the airport and headed for the offsite agency my thoughts were, "My God, I'll never find this place when we get back."

"Have you ever driven in this country before?" the young woman asked.

"Yes," I replied. "A number of times. It usually takes me fifteen or twenty minutes to get reoriented."

"We had a Spanish gentleman in here last week who didn't get off of the lot before he had hit two different cars," she said.

"I can appreciate his difficulty," I responded. "It takes some getting used to."

I was directed to a Daewoo; pee green in color and a little larger than I had expected. John went through all of the features with me and wished us a happy holiday. We placed our bags in the boot, my golf clubs in the back seat and started from the lot; extremely carefully, I might add. John had pointed out that the car had only one-fourth a tank of petrol and, if I were going far, I would need petrol. There was a petrol station across the street. No matter how many times I have driven in Europe, the first petrol fill-up is always a shock. Petrol was selling for 76 pence a liter. It takes

3.79 liters to make a gallon, so petrol sells for the American equivalent of about $2.90 a gallon. My first fill-up cost about $48.00. One does not see SUVs in Europe.

The first challenge is effectively getting out of the city. Driving from the right side of the car on the left side of the road is a challenge. But starting out in the city, with cars parked along the streets and trying to emerge from the roundabout on the same road by which one went into it, takes a lot of patience and total concentration. Jane and I knew we had to drive approximately 200 miles this first day. We had allowed ourselves six hours for this drive. We had planned to drive up through the center of Scotland on the A-81, so that we could enjoy the countryside and small villages along the way. The A-81 is a two lane road that snakes through the center of this beautiful country. We left Glasgow about 1:30pm and at 3:00pm we realized that we had covered about 40 miles. At this rate it would be well after dark when we reached our destination ánd we do not like to drive in strange countries, on strange roads, on strange sides of roads, after dark. We consulted our map and headed for the most direct route from where we were, toward Inverness; which was the A-9.

For Americans old enough to have driven before the Interstate highways system, an A road in the UK is like the old intrastate routes. They are primarily two lane roads, occasionally expanded into "dual carriageways" (four lanes) to allow for the passing of slower traffic like, trucks, buses, or farm equipment. Since this was harvest season, as the day worn on, more tractors presented themselves on the road as they headed home at the end of the workday. The "dual carriageways" are usually only two to five miles in length, so there is not a great deal of high speed driving.

What one immediately notices when driving in Europe generally and Scotland specifically is the absence of outdoor advertising. One can see panoramic views of the countryside without the visual pollution of billboards. The A-9 wended its way northward through valleys between tree covered mountains that gave way to valleys between rocky, treeless mountains, into still more valleys with stone farm houses and meadows filled with sheep. The lochs of the north began to appear. It was no less a pretty drive than the one we had planned. It took us three hours to travel about 120 miles and as we crossed the great bridge in Inverness heading further north toward Tain, the sun was low in the sky. We reached the Golf View Guest House at 6:30pm. It was dark at 6:40pm.

Ian and Rae Ross, our hosts, had converted a former vicarage into a beautiful house at the edge of the village of Tain, overlooking a large meadow and, in the distance, the Tain Golf Course. I had stayed with Ian and Rae on a previous trip so I knew that the accommodations would be excellent. Jane and I were given the room in which I had stayed previously. Since it was now dark, Jane was not able to see the view but I knew that in the morning, we would be looking out of our window over the fields toward the firth.

We were tired and hungry. There was no need to drive in Tain so we walked down to the village center, passed the Royal Hotel to the St. Duthus Hotel. To an

American, hotel conjures up Hilton or Marriott. The St. Duthus Hotel has rooms and a dining room in which to eat. At 8:00pm things were quiet. In fact, on our walk to the hotel, we saw few people on the street. In the dining area, two women were sitting together talking over drinks and a family of four was just finishing a meal. A pretty teenage girl brought us menus and took our drink orders. As we often do, Jane and I wondered about her life in this small village in northern Scotland. Would she ever leave here? Would she ever *want* to leave? I ordered a gamon steak with boiled potatoes and Jane ordered a large bowl of corn chowder, which, to her surprise, also came with a bowl of boiled potatoes. I ordered my first pint of lager. Jane ordered a white wine. She later opined that she wished she had ordered the lager.

As we walked back to our guesthouse, we smelled in the evening air a smell that had been absent from our lives since childhood; the smell of coal smoke. On this chilly evening in mid October, the local residents were heating their houses in the way their ancestors had for several hundred years, with coal. It is one of those never to be forgotten smells that, through the mystery of the senses, transports one back through decades to a different time and a different place when long forgotten smells were ordinary. We walked into our past down the gray, stone streets of Tain and enjoyed the mystic transportation on a carpet of coal smoke. We had had a long day. Sleep was not far off. It was a fitting end to day two of our holiday.

Day Three

A single golfer has two options: one is to go to a golf course at anytime and seek to be paired with others to fill out a three ball or four ball. A second option is to try to get a tee time as a single and let the golf professional pair someone with you. Since my tee times had been arranged as a single, I often had the earliest tee times of the day, the later times being reserved for club members and larger groups. In the spring and summer, this is not often a problem, since the sun rises early in the northern hemisphere and sets late. In the fall, however, the earliest tee times are for the dew sweepers. My tee time at the Royal Dornoch Golf Club was 7:50am. Europeans, generally, are not early risers. Breakfast is nearly always after 8:00am. Ian and Don, however, keep golfers so they agreed to have breakfast for Jane and me at 6:30am. A Bed and Breakfast serves a full Scottish breakfast: cereal with milk and fruit, followed by hot porridge, followed by bacon, sausage, eggs, mushrooms, broiled tomato, toast with marmalade, and coffee. Since golf courses are to be walked, (if a golf course has a riding cart, one has to have a doctor's assertion of disability to use it) one fortifies oneself with this hearty breakfast knowing it will soon be burned off through exercise. Jane, who normally nibbles on the edge of a piece of toast for breakfast, with her gallon of coffee, was overwhelmed. I urged this bodily fortification on her.

(On earlier trips to Scotland, few golf courses had riding carts, or buggies as they are called locally. One had to have a doctor's assertion of disability to use a buggy, if one was available. Now, however, many courses have buggies to rent, usually to Americans who have not walked a golf course in their golfing career.)

It was still twilight when we left the Golf View Guest House for the fifteen-minute drive to Dornoch. The Royal Dornoch Golf Club is my favorite golf course in Scotland. The game has been played on these links since the early 1600s. The panoramic views and gorse-lined fairways combine to present to the golfer one of the world's beautiful golf courses. In the spring, when the gorse is in bloom, the yellow of the gorse and the blue of the Firth outline each fairway and green. On this October morning, however, the gorse was not in bloom, the Firth was not blue, there was a spit of rain in the air, and the wind was adjusting the flags aligning the first tee to a ninety-degree angle. This was going to be Jane's first test of golf in Scotland. I confess that I was concerned that as this day went, so would the rest of the holiday. I reported to the pro shop.

"Mr. Coomer, the person who was to play with you this morning has cancelled," said the young man behind the counter.

I glanced at Jane, who said nothing aloud but her look said, "Why am I not surprised?"

Jane had layered her clothing for this outing but had nothing to wear on her head.

"I think we need to buy you a cap," I said.

She looked around for something that would be acceptable in which to be seen, although we would be the only two on the course this early. She selected a navy and gray cap with the Royal Dornoch logo on it. I could tell she was thinking, "What will this do to my hair?"

We headed to the starter's shed on the first tee. I was so excited about playing that I had forgotten to put on my golf shoes. When I returned to the tee from the car after changing my shoes, Jane and the starter, a wizened little man in a woolen cap, were chatting amiably. I began to swing a club back and forth to loosen up a few joints.

"You've played here before, haven't you, sir," the starter said to me.

"Yes, I have."

"I thought I recognized you," he said.

I smiled. The last time I had played there had been four and a half years ago.

"Do you remember the blind tee shots on 7 and 17? Stay to the left. Play away."

The first hole is a short, 331-yard par four. The wind was behind us attempting to blow Jane off of the teeing area. Hoping to hit the fairway with my first swing of the day, I chose to hit a seven wood. I hit it high and to the right.

"You can reach the green from there," opined the starter as he headed for the warmth of his shed.

Jane and I were off: nae wind, nae rain, nae golf. As we marched down the first four fairways, Jane noticed that several people were bringing their dogs

43

down through the course toward the beach for their morning runs and morning business. It was not a sight she had seen on many U.S. golf courses. The first eight holes at Royal Dornoch Golf Club hug the gorse-covered ridge that runs along the left side of the course. The houses perched along the road on that ridge have breathtaking views of the golf course and the Dornoch Firth. The wind was behind us on these first eight holes and I managed three pars and one birdie on these holes. The fifth hole, named Hilton, is reputed to be Tom Watson's favorite hole on the course. It is played from an elevated tee, over the gorse, between and among eight pot bunkers. My favorite hole is the par 3 sixth hole named, Whinny Brae. It is a short, 163-yard hole with the gorse-covered ridge the entire length on the left with an abrupt drop off to the right of the green. If one successfully hits the ball down the ridgeline to the left of the green one finds, when reaching the green, three small pot bunkers unseen from the tee box. If one misses the green to the right, the ball goes down an incline. Such is golf in Scotland.

The eighth green sits at the shoreline of the Firth and from there one plays nine of the next ten holes along the coastline back toward the clubhouse. The seventeenth hole, with its blind tee shot, one of which the starter reminded me, reverses direction but only for this one hole. When the weather is nice, these are extraordinarily beautiful golf holes. On this morning, however, when Jane and I turned into the wind, score was forgotten; survival took precedence. I was having a great time. Jane was trying to keep her new cap on her head, by pulling the hood of her jacket over it and, I suspected, began counting how many holes there were yet to be played. As we walked the eighteenth fairway, the sun broke through the clouds and a gigantic rainbow appeared. We could see it from end to end; too lengthy for a picture but it was an omen for the week to come.

Sitting next to the clubhouse of the Royal Dornoch Golf Club is the Royal Golf Hotel, with its glass windowed lounge looking out over the first fairway. Soup, sandwich, and a pint in the warmth of this room were my reward to Jane for her morning workout. One of the windows in the dining area, facing the first fairway, was cracked. Someone had created a computer-generated poster and taped it to the broken window. It read:

A really
Good
Shot Would Have Broken
Both Panes

I asked our waiter how often one of the windows got broken. He told us this one was only the second in thirteen years. He then revealed that it was the golfer's third shot off of the #1 teeing area that hit the window. Because of how the hotel is sited, to hit this window a golfer would have had to duck-hook his tee shot from the championship tees. I told Jane that I suspected that his first two shots had gone way to the right and he said to himself, "dammit, I'm not going to hit this one right." He didn't. He hit it way left.

Hanging on lines stretched across the ceiling of the bar in the Royal Golf Hotel are hundreds of golf bag tags from golf courses around the world. The last time I was here I donated my bag tag in exchange for a pint. Hundreds of other golfers have done the same. This may be one of the unique collections in the world.

By having such an early tee time, Jane and I now had the afternoon free to wander about. There was too much to see in the area during one afternoon but that is usually the way of things when one is on holiday.

The town of Dornoch boasts two names with which many Americans are familiar; Andrew Carnegie and Donald Ross. Although Andrew Carnegie was born in Dunfermline, Scotland's capital until 1603, he retired to the area of Dornoch where he built the "castle of his dreams" at Skibo. In retirement, Carnegie and his wife decided to take up golf and he became vice-President of the Royal Dornoch Golf Club. His memory is also perpetuated in the Dornoch Cathedral, in the center of the town, by three stained glass windows representing the interests of his retirement years – Learning, Peace, and Music. In 1979, the cathedral organ was completely rebuilt through the generosity of Carnegie's daughter.

Donald Ross, although lesser known by non-golfers than Andrew Carnegie, was born in Dornoch, learning to play golf on the Dornoch links and learning to make golf clubs under the direction of Old Tom Morris in St. Andrews. Ross, like Carnegie, also immigrated to America where he established himself as one of the great golf course architects. Oakland Hills in Michigan,

Oak Hill in New York, Inverness in Ohio, Pinehurst #2 in North Carolina, and the Broadmoor in Colorado are only a well known few of the 400 golf courses he designed in the United States. In Knoxville, Tennessee, where my wife and I attended university, there is a Donald Ross course; Holston Hills. A little of the Dornoch links are to be found in each them.

The Cathedral one visits in the heart of the town of Dornoch has a foundation established in the year 1224. The present Cathedral is the result of restoration began in the 19th century and stained glass windows and organ added in the 20th century. Jane and I have visited a number of churches and cathedrals throughout Europe but the intimacy of this beautiful building attracted us immediately. To travel 6,000 miles to play golf in this Royal Burgh is a pleasure, but to drive past this Cathedral, to and from the links, without stopping for a brief visit is to miss an experience as equally moving as a good round of golf. The town, the Cathedral, and the links combine to place a mantel of 700 years of history about the shoulders of any visitor. It is a warm and comforting feeling.

Several miles to the north of Dornoch is the village of Golspie in which is located Dunrobin Castle, the ancestral home of the Earls of Sutherland. This strikingly beautiful, 189 room castle sits high above the Dornoch Firth and the grounds between the castle and the beach have been transformed into beautifully designed gardens. The literature one reads about the castle informs the visitor that the gardens were laid out in 1850, inspired by those at Versailles, and have been altered little in the 150 years since they were planted. The castle is one of Britain's oldest continuously inhabited houses, dating in part from the early 1300s. The last Duke of Sutherland, though having two wives, died "without issue" in the late 20th century so the lands and title passed to, I am sure, a pleasantly surprised other branch of the family. The views from the rooms of the castle out over the gardens and firth are magnificent. As is always the case, Jane and I are amazed at the splendor of these ancient homes. Dunrobin Castle was well worth the visit.

Gardens of Dunrobin Castle, Village of Golspie

With about three hours of daylight left on this sunny but windy afternoon, Jane and I had to decide where to spend the rest of the day. We had three choices. One was a visit to the Glenmorangie Distillery. A second choice was to the Falls of Shin to see if any salmon were leaping. The third was to the Tain Pottery, one of Scotland's largest ceramic manufactures. We decided to visit them as we came upon them. The first, by happy coincidence, was the distillery. Although we did not meet personally with "The Sixteen Men of Tain," the mashmen, stillmen, and warehousemen who are entrusted with crafting the singular taste of Glenmorangie Single Highland Scotch Malt Whisky, we did learn the process by which malt whisky is created; from malting the barley grains, to drying the barley, to mashing the ground malt, to fermentation when adding yeast, to distillation, to aging in oak casks. After absorbing all of this information, we then absorbed a wee dram of the product. We were impressed enough that, for the remainder of our trip, we occasionally ordered a wee dram at various other locations about the country.

Time dictated that we forgo the Falls of Shin and try to visit the Tain Pottery before they closed for the day. We were too late to see the pottery shaped and fired in the kilns but we did see examples of the various designs and different series of chargers, teapots, jugs, breakfast cups and saucers, and casseroles. Each an original design and all hand painted. I discouraged Jane from shipping the Kirksheaf collection to our home. I encouraged her to contribute to the local economy in a more practical way, sipping some more Glenmorangie single malt scotch.

Darkness was falling as we head toward the Golf View Guest House. On our way, we past the Morangie

House Hotel, which is located at the opposite end of Tain from our lodgings. I made a quick U-turn and, upon checking the posted menu, booked a table for dinner. After a brief rest and a change of clothes, we discovered that we had made the right decision. It was a pleasant and relaxing evening after a full day of activity. Day three of our holiday, although starting out cold and wet, ended with warmth and an anticipation of an enjoyable week to come.

Day Four

Whereas day two was our longest day drive north, day four was to be our longest day drive south. We were to meet our friends Neil and Agnes Morton in Perth at 11:30am. Tain to Perth is approximately 125 miles, so we allowed three hours for the drive. Rae and Ian Ross, our hosts at the Golf View Guest House, provided a 7:30am breakfast and a few minutes after 8:00am we were back on the A-9 retracing our previous route. It was a beautiful, fall, Saturday morning with temperatures in the mid-50s (f). The sky was clear, the traffic tolerable, and the scenery outstanding. I assume because of the climate, Great Britain and Ireland have more hues of the color green than any other place we have ever traveled. With Bach's melodic *The Sheep Shall Safely Graze* on the fringe of consciousness, we wandered back south through the glens, stone-walls, ruined castles, and working farms of the Scottish Highlands toward the ancient city of Perth.

The city of Perth, with its mid-size population of 50,000 and its central location in the country, served in times past as Scotland's capital. Forty-two Scottish Kings were crowned on the Stone of Destiny in this city. It is now renowned for its parks and gardens. It is within an hours drive of Edinburgh and Glasgow and, for the golfer, a thirty minute drive to St. Andrews or Carnoustie.

With only one wrong turn, we arrived at the Dunallan Guest House at 11:00am. We were shown into a bright, comfortable looking room on the first floor (one floor above the ground floor) with a large bay window looking down on the street. I hurriedly filled the electric pot to heat water and make a cup of tea. By previous arrangement, Neil Morton had invited me to play golf at his club and his wife, Agnes, and Jane were going to spend the day sightseeing and shopping. We would meet for dinner in the evening. Neil and I left in his car. Jane and Agnes would travel by taxi.

My first golfing trip to Scotland was with the planning and assistance of Neil and Agnes Morton, who owned Morton Golf. The trip was everything that I had hoped it would be and each subsequent trip, therefore, was coordinated through Neil and Agnes. In 2004, Neil and Agnes sold Morton Golf to Peter and Fiona Craigon. I have subsequently worked with Peter and Fiona and I can, and will, testify to the fact that Peter and Fiona have continued to build Morton Golf on the foundation of personal service laid down by Neil and Agnes. Anyone planning a golfing trip to Scotland would do well to allow themselves to be guided by these knowledgeable and enthusiastic golfers. (info.mortongolf.com)

The River Tay runs through the city of Perth. It is a tidal river and, although it is several miles from the coast, seals can frequently be seen swimming the river around the city. Within in the city of Perth, in the middle of the River Tay, is an island and on that island is the King James VI Golf Club. King James VI of Scotland, son of Mary Queen of Scots, later became

King James I of England, succeeding Elizabeth I, daughter of Henry VIII. The present Golf Club dates from 1858, so King James I never played it but, like so many golf courses in Scotland, golf has been played on this site for such a long period of time so, perhaps he did.

The golf course is accessed by parking behind a deserted geriatric hospital and walking along an elevated walkway, beside the railroad tracks, that takes one across a trestle over the Tay and down a series of steps to a pathway that leads to the golf course clubhouse. The course is neither long (6038 yards from the medal tees) nor difficult, but it is unique. The course has been flooded by an overflowing Tay in the past and Neil told me that on several occasions, when the river was at it highest, boats passing near the course would cause the water in their wake to wash up onto greens bordering the river.

The weather was warm, low 60s(f) and I played in a long sleeved shirt and a wind vest. I noticed a few natives in short sleeved shirts but they were far hardier than I. It was an enjoyable experience and a forgettable round.

Jane and Agnes, meanwhile, were shopping and visiting Scone Palace, the home of the Earls of Mansfield. The palace was built on the site of an abbey destroyed by followers of John Knox in 1559. Those impetuous Protestants! Between the 9th and 13th centuries, Scone guarded the sacred Stone of Destiny on which the Scottish kings were crowned. The stone is now kept in Edinburgh Castle. A collection worth seeing in this palace is the porcelain. One can also see the bed hangings worked on my Mary Queen of Scots. As are nearly all of the great houses of Europe, the palace is surrounded by over 100 acres of gardens and woodland walkways. The gardens of these lovely castles, in Scotland and in England, are wonderful places in which to wander and wonder at the beauty and variety of flowers seemingly perpetually in bloom.

When Neil and I returned from the King James VI Golf Club at about 5:00pm, Jane was sitting in the lounge of our guesthouse, sipping tea and anxious to talk about her day's activities. Neil and Agnes were going to pick us up for dinner at 7:00pm so we chatted as we dressed. The four of us are of a generation that still dresses when we go out to dinner. Jane and I had noticed that, during the past few years, the American casualness of dress had invaded Europe. We had expected and accepted the casual dress at hotels near golf courses but in the finer restaurants of the cities we were often surprised at the dress of other diners. Neil, when I asked, said that he would wear a coat and tie to dinner because, "that is just the way I am." I was delighted to know that Jane and I would not be overdressed for the occasion.

European cities abound with small, intimate restaurants. Our evening with Neil and Agnes was in such a setting. We sat, as friends and acquaintances have sat for thousands of years, over bread. We ate well, we drank wine, we laughed, and we talked. Jane and I thanked them for helping us plan this holiday. I took their picture in front of the restaurant before they left us to walk to their home. Jane and I took a taxi back to our guesthouse. We were 125 miles from where we had started the day, but it had been a day filled with a variety of activities. Day four of our holiday ended as it had begun, with good food. It had been a good day.

Day Five

Day five, Sunday morning, began with a crisis; Jane could not find her reading glasses. Like many people generally, and a number of women specifically, Jane believes glasses to be utilitarian, not a fashion statement. While I often drop my glasses into the breast pocket of a jacket, Jane often places hers on the nearest hard surface.

"When is the last time you remember having them?" I asked.

"I am sure I had them when we left for dinner last night...I think," she responded.

"Are you positive?"

"I think that I am positive."

I let that affirmation sink in. "Do you remember reading the menu with them?"

"I am not sure. Yes I am. I remember now that I did not have them at dinner. I had to borrow Agnes' glasses, which encouraged you to tell that George Allen story.

Years before, in Washington, D.C., Jane and I were having dinner at the Washington Hilton Hotel on Connecticut Avenue when a man at the next table asked Jane if he could borrow her glasses so that he could read the menu. She immediately obliged and the man placed her half-glasses on his nose and ordered from the menu. He thanked her and returned the glasses.

"Do you know who that man is?" I asked her.

"I haven't the slightest idea," she responded.

"That's George Allen, the coach of the Washington Redskins football team."

"Oh," was her only response.

As a long time Washington Redskins fan dating back to my early days in Washington D.C. when the Washington Redskins football team and the Washington Senators baseball team played their games in Griffith Stadium and our quarterback, Ralph Gugliemi, was the team's second leading ground gainer for the season from having to run out of the pocket so much, I was obviously more impressed with this intimate encounter with the legendary Allen than was my wife.

"Did you have them when you were shopping this afternoon?"

"Yes. I am sure that I did."

"Well, in that case, they could be most anywhere," I surmised wanting to be helpful but mindful of the fact that I had a 9:30am tee time.

"I have searched the room, floor to ceiling, and the entire luggage. They are not here."

"Well, I don't know anything else to suggest," I ventured. "If you didn't read the menu with them, there is no sense in calling the restaurant."

"I thought that I had them at Neil and Agnes' but I honestly can't be sure."

"If they find them, they will send them to us."

The day was not beginning well. St. Andrews was about a thirty minute drive from Perth and the Kingsbarns Golf Links, where I was scheduled to play, was six miles south of St. Andrews. I reasoned that if we left the Dunallan Guest House by 8:15am, I could drive to Kingsbarns by 9:00am, plenty of time to spare. We crossed the Tay Bridge and headed toward the most well-known venue in golf, a name known to golfers and non-golfers alike as the undisputed home of the game: St. Andrews. Although the Sunday morning traffic was sparse, the narrow roads and small villages stretched the 30-mile drive into an hour. After one wrong turn, I arrived in the Kingsbarns parking area at 9:15am.

Although its history dates from 1783, Kingsbarns Golf Links was reborn at the turn of the 21st century. Because of the terrain, the area of the golf course, like several other links venues, was commandeered for military purposes during the Second World War. Since then, several efforts were undertaken to recapture and to recreate this beautiful stretch of ground into a championship golf course. In the few years since its rebirth, Kingsbarns has become a "must play" for golfers when coming to the St. Andrews area. The scenery is spectacular; the sea is always in view and, as often as possible within "the frame of play – behind greens, in front of the greens, directly behind driving lines, and often hazarding an aggressive line of play." The layout of the course along the firth and the vistas from the course remind me a great deal of Royal Dornoch.

I reported to the starter. Jane headed to find a hot cup of coffee. The weather continued to be accommodating; high 50s(f). Two young men introduced themselves to me as my playing partners.

They were, it turned out, from Boston, Massachusetts and their first question to me after the introductions was, "Have you heard any playoff (baseball) scores?" The New York Yankees were playing the Boston Red Sox for the opportunity of playing in the World Series. I had to confess that I had not. The BBC could keep me abreast of cricket, soccer, and snooker results but not American baseball scores. These young men had been in Scotland for a week and were having the time of their lives. They had played the Old Course the day before and Carnoustie the day before that. Kingsbarns was their final round of golf before driving to Edinburgh to begin their flight home. They could not have finished their golfing trip on a finer venue.

The starter had presented to each of us, including Jane (whom he thought was a player), a small tartan bag to attach to our golf bags in which we found a score card, a pencil, a course guide, tees, a ball marker, and an implement with which to repair ball marks on the greens. He told us the best line for ball flight on the first hole was down the left side of the fairway. He instructed us to play away and each of us promptly hit the ball down the right side of the fairway; so much for instruction.

I had not played three holes at Kingsbarns before concluding that this was going to be a great experience. The course guide suggested options for playing each hole; "aggressive drives, successfully executed, open up advantageous angles to approach the greens." Safe driving, on the other hand, even though one's ball was in the fairway, often presented a second shot that upon hitting the ground, or the green, did not move in an anticipated direction. The large greens seemed to be divided into a series of smaller greens and, even when reaching the green in regulation, the position of the ball vis-à-vis the position of the flagstick, often required tentative and defensive putting. I am a reasonably good putter and I putted very well this day.

Jane was walking the course with us and thoroughly enjoying this beautiful environment. As we walked up the ninth fairway, a young man approached Jane and asked, "Are you the lady who has lost her glasses?"

Jane looked at him bewildered and replied, "Yes, I am."

"Your friends are bringing them to you and will meet you in the clubhouse at 1:30."

Jane met me on the green. "Neil and Agnes found my glasses and are bringing them over to me. They will be here about 1:30."

"What time is it now?" I asked.

"11:40," she replied.

"That will be just about right," I calculated.

The twelfth hole at Kingsbarns, the longest, plays 606 yards from the championship tees and 566 yards from the medal tees. It is followed by the shortest hole on the course, 135 yards, with the smallest green. There is a large rock to the left of this green and five bunkers surrounding the green. With the wind directly behind us, one of my playing partners hit a pitching wedge over the green. I reasoned that I was between clubs and, since the front of the green was 107 yards, I decided to hit a 52degree gap wedge thinking that I would at least be able to hit on the front of the green. That is exactly where my ball landed, on the right front of the green. As I was putting my club back into my bag, Jane said, "Look!" I looked and saw my ball begin to move ever so slightly toward the edge of the green. It picked up momentum and, in a moment, had disappeared into the mouth of a small pot bunker. "Oh, well," I thought, "the worst I should get is a four." I climbed down into the bunker and executed a decent bunker shot. The ball landed about three feet onto the putting surface. "Two putts for a bogie," I thought. I'll take it.

"Look!" said Jane again. The ball began to roll, imperceptive at first then, picking up speed, rolled into an enormous bunker adjacent to the one from which I thought I had just extracted my ball. From this second bunker, I had to look almost straight up toward the green. I opened the face of a sand wedge and hit the ball straight up in the air. The ball landed on the edge of the green and, before I could move from the spot, proceeded to return itself to my feet. Not wanting to spend the day in this bunker, I hit my fourth shot on this short par-3 hole well past the flagstick and two putted for a six. Beware of the shortest holes on a golf course.

On the sixteenth fairway, Jane left us to meet the Mortons at the clubhouse. My Boston companions and I played on. The finishing hole at Kingsbarns is a 444yard par 4 with a surprise. A good drive will allow the golfer to see the 18th green but not what is lurking below it. Without a course guide, the first time player is not aware that a small burn (tributary of water) lies out of sight at the foot of the rise on which the green sits. As the course guide warns, "Anything just short of the green is likely to find the burn and a fast ride out to sea." I decided to hit my second shot short of the burn, hit a wedge close to the pin, and one putt for a par. I did hit my second shot short of the burn. I did hit a wedge to the green. I did not one putt for a par. My first, and I sincerely hope it is only my first, round of golf at Kingsbarns Golf Links was a truly delightful experience.

I bade good-bye to my playing partners and hurried to the clubhouse for another visit with Neil and Agnes. We had a memorable lunch together in the clubhouse. It was memorable because I was offered a choice of one of three cheeses on my burger. One choice was Stilton. Although I love Stilton cheese, I had never expected to eat it on a burger. I think that I will not make a similar choice until I am next at Kingsbarns.

Our bonus for the day was spending more time with Agnes and Neil and talking about Scottish golf courses yet to be played and countryside and villages yet to be visited on future trips. We again said our good byes and Jane and I made the turn toward St. Andrews for an afternoon of leisurely sightseeing.

Finding a place to park in St. Andrews at any time is problematic but on a Sunday afternoon in October with temperatures in the low 60s(f) it is nearly impossible. I knew approximately where our guesthouse was located and was lucky to find a parking space about a block away. We pulled our bags to the door only to find a note posted there that read, in order to check in, call a telephone number listed on the card. Damn. Now I need to find a call box and I had to have change. Jane waited with the bags while I went in search of a call box. The irritation, like most irritations, was the inconvenience of not having something when one wants it. The remedy was not difficult. I found a call box, called the posted number, and a delightful voice said that she would be there "straight away." When I returned to Jane, a large van was exiting a parking space directly across the street from our guest house. I doubted that the space would be vacant for a long period of time. I ran to where we had parked our car and hurriedly drove around the block. The space was still there, with Jane doing everything but lying down in it to prevent someone else from taking it. By the time I had parked, our hostess had arrived.

There were about three and a half hours of daylight left and I wanted Jane to see this quaint little town. One can easily walk the length and breadth of St. Andrews but there is a great deal to see. We walked down Market Street and decided that we should do our obligatory shopping before the stores closed. We could not return from St. Andrews without golf shirts for our daughter and son-in-law. One does not get maximum use out of sweaters in Atlanta and although the selections of beautiful sweaters are tempting, they are not practical where we live. We decided on cotton shirts with the Old Course logo on them and once that was done, our shopping was done.

I walked Jane through the parking lot of the Royal and Ancient Clubhouse so that her first view of the Old Course would be the 18th green and the combined 1st and 18th fairways with the public road running through them.

Royal and Ancient Clubhouse, St. Andrews

By tradition, the Old Course is closed on Sundays (although the New Course and the Jubilee Course which share the peninsula are opened.) What Jane saw was scores of people walking down the fairways of the Old Course, some walking their dogs; students wandering the course hand in hand; tourists peeking in the windows of the R&A clubhouse; people having their pictures taken on the Swilken Bridge (we waited for our turn); and generally using this venerable piece of ground as a public park.

Jane on the Swilkin Bridge, Old Course, St. Andrews

She was, to say the least, surprised. We wandered down to the 17th green. The hole is named simply, Road, because the green sits within ten yards of a road and, contrary to USGA rules which allows "nearest point of relief," when a golfer playing this hole finds his golf ball on the road, the ball must be played as it lies; from the road.

17th hole, "The Road Hole", Old Course, St. Andrews

From the road and across the green lies the famous, or infamous, Road Hole bunker. Anyone who has ever watched a golf tournament played at St. Andrews has witnessed the agony of some of the best golfers in the world as they attempt to extract their ball from this bunker. It is not an infrequent occurrence that it takes more strokes to get out of the bunker than it took to get in. The other interesting feature of this hole is that the desired line of flight for the ball driven from the teeing area is directly over a series of sheds that are built out behind the Old Course Hotel that borders this hole. The last time that I played this course I received appreciable applause from three women standing nearby who witnessed my successful drive directly over the sheds and into the fairway. Since the Old Course is a public course, it is not unusual for one playing the course to be followed for a few holes by walkers who are heading to the beach or who are simply walking along the fringes of the course.

Jane, as a non-golfer, was singularly unimpressed with the Old Course. Its unkempt appearance, its parallel fairways, its large double greens, and its relative flatness, (in addition to it doubling as a public park on Sundays) was not what she had been expecting. Royal Dornoch and Kingsbarns were much more beautiful. She appreciated the history, even the difficulty of playing this course in the wind and rain (while she would be sitting snuggly in the clubhouse with coffee and a book), but the Old Course was just an old course to her. For me the golfer, however, the course is not seen for its beauty; it is seen for its magic.

It isn't just the fact that every known golfer in the world has played this course, it is that thousands of unknown golfers over hundreds of years have hacked away on these links and their ghosts, with their love for the game, follow each succeeding generation of golfers down these fairways, smiling at the lies, chuckling at those cursing the weather, exulting over the great bunker shots, nodding in agreement with club selection, and shaking their heads at poor shot execution. "Been there, laddie,...had that shot," seems to be a part of the atmosphere of every hole. I love playing this course because I believe the daily galleries number in the hundreds of thousands. I want to play well for them and to receive their approval.

At the golf courses most Americans associate with St. Andrews, the Old, the New, and the Jubilee courses, there are two clubhouses; the ever-present Royal and Ancient Clubhouse and the generally unphotographed links clubhouse.

The Royal and Ancient Clubhouse is, arguably, the best know golf clubhouse in the world. It is for members only. It has continuous records dating from 1754 and Royal patronage was conferred in 1834. The present R&A Clubhouse was built in 1854. There are 1800 members worldwide. On previous trips to the St. Andrews Links, through the auspices of an acquaintance who is a member, I have been a Temporary Member of the R & A with the privileges of using the locker room, eating in the dining room, and enjoying the comfort and hospitality afforded in The Big Room, with its windows facing onto the 1st and 18th

fairways. A jacket and tie are a requirement in The Big Room. The members of the R & A whom I have met when using their Clubhouse have been welcoming and convivial hosts. Sitting in The Big Room, sipping a gin and tonic while writing a letter to Jane on the blue R&A stationery is one of the memorable pleasures of my golfing experiences in Scotland.

On this Sunday afternoon in October, however, Jane and I went to the St. Andrews Links clubhouse for a cup of tea and to enjoy the environment. Sitting in this clubhouse is like sitting in an international airport. One sees golfers from around the world and hears them replaying their rounds in the languages of the world. The universality of the game, with its common language and general rules, creates, in this place, a community of like-minded people who have traveled thousands of miles to share a common experience in an uncommon environment. Their pleasure is palpable. Strangers make eye contact. Nods are exchanged. It is a wonderful place just to sit and sip tea.

With daylight dwindling, I wanted Jane to see more than just the golf course. We wandered through Scotland's oldest university town, through the university and medieval churches, toward the ruins of the 12th-century cathedral at the edge of the town. The shell of this once massive building is as impressive in its ruin as it must have been when it was the largest cathedral in Scotland.

Remains of the Cathedral at St. Andrews

St. Andrew's Castle, built in 1200, commands an imposing view out over St. Andrew's Bay. The dungeons in this castle, in which a number of religious Reformers were held, can still be seen. We wandered into the Parish Church of the Holy Trinity. Evening services were about ready to begin in a small chapel off of the Nave. An elderly couple came up to us and, when learning we were tourists just wanting to see their church, obliged us with a wonderful history of the building, built in 1412, which boast some beautiful windows. Like many churches in Europe, the walls are filled with memorials to notable members whose families wished them to be remembered in perpetuity. The organ in this small church is reputed to be among the finest in Scotland and, as we were wandering with our guides, we were treated to the wonderful sounds of this instrument as it accompanied the evening hymns. There is a memorial to Tom Morris, whom I assumed was either Old Tom or Young Tom, the famous golfers. It was in this church that John Knox preached his first sermon in public. That occasion is also recognized in an inscription on the John Knox Porch of the church, which reads "In this town and church began God's first calling to the dignity of the preacher." We were told that Knox also preached one of his last sermons in this church. It is surprising what one can learn by simply pushing open a door for a peek inside. It was at this church on July 11, 1617 that the Rector of St. Andrews University delivered a Latin address of welcome to King James VI upon his visit to his old Kingdom of Scotland. Our interest in old churches had seldom been rewarded with such serendipitous pleasure.

As Jane and I wandered back toward our guesthouse, we began to read the posted menus in restaurants along the way. We both knew that this was going to be a light meal evening followed by a good night's sleep. We settled on soup, bread, and cheese, accompanied by a couple of gin and tonics, made one more pass in homage to the Old Course, and called it a day. We could not have crowded one more thing into our fifth day.

Day Six

While we were planning this trip, Jane and I wanted to be tourists as much as golfers. As much as I regretted not playing the Old Course on this trip, I did not want to spend an extra day in St. Andrews just to do it. Our plans called for us to spend day six in Edinburgh. Edinburgh is approximately fifty miles from St. Andrews, which allowed us a leisurely morning to linger over breakfast and coffee. I wanted to arrive in Edinburgh early enough for us to enjoy a full day of activities but not so early that I would be driving in with the morning commuters. I get unnerved driving in the U.S. during rush hour. Driving from the right on the left in unfamiliar surroundings is stressful. Our first stop, however, was at the first petrol station; ($53.27equivalent US dollars). That certainly cut into our lunch options. Approaching Edinburgh, I simply followed the signs toward the City Centre where I planned to park for the day.

"There's a parking space," said Jane.

"Damn." In my too hasty turn toward the curbing, my over-the-left-front perception failed me and I bounced off of the curb. As it turned out, we were at the entrance to a parking garage and, not knowing the restriction regarding on-street parking, I opted for the parking garage. As I took my ticket and headed into the bowels of the parking deck I said, "I think we have a flat tire." I found a space in which to park and got out to check for damage. The left front tire was flat. My hasty turn to the curb had sliced a three inch cut into the tire wall. I was of two minds; irritated at my own ineptitude and grateful that, in all of my driving in Great Britain, this was my first casualty; and a minor one at that. I found a parking garage attendant and explained my dilemma. He suggested that I call the AA (Automobile Association) and was able to provide me with a telephone number. I found a call box on the street and called the AA.

"I am a tourist in a hired car. I am in the Castle Terrace car park and I have a flat tire. Could you send one to change it?"

"Are you a member of AA?"

"I am a member of AAA in the U.S. Is that helpful?"

"No, sir. We can, however, send someone out to change the tire for 85 pounds."

"85 pounds!" I exclaimed incredulously as my mind did the arithmetic. That was $150 to change a tire. "Never mind," I said. "I'll change it myself."

Jane, ever helpful, offered a suggestion. "Why don't you look at our rental contract to see if our company has offices here?"

I did and it did. I walked back to the call box.

"Arnold Clarke Toyota," said a male voice.

"I have a hired car from Arnold Clarke and I am in the Castle Terrace parking garage with a flat tire. Do you have a service that can come over to change a tire?"

"Where did you hire the car?"

"Glasgow."

"Then you will have to call Glasgow."

"But, what good will that do? I am in Edinburgh."

"Glasgow is our central service center."

"Won't they simply refer me to someone in Edinburgh?"

"Just a moment, sir."

Using a public call box in Europe is neither for the uninitiated nor is it for an unlimited period of time. One must be prepared to feed the machine acceptable coinage for the amount of time one is on line. In anticipation of this, I had placed a pound coin in the slot to insure maximum time. My concern was that if this young man did not get back to me quickly, I would be disconnected and would then have to find more coins with which to begin the process all over again.

"Sir," the voice returned. "What is the registration number of your vehicle?" I had the contract in hand and could supply it readily. "And your name?" I also knew the answer to that question. "We will have someone there within thirty minutes."

"Thank you very much," I said. "I am on deck two, space 85."

Jane and I returned to the garage and I began to unload the boot in order to get to the spare tire. In about thirty minutes a small truck pulled up beside us with AA painted on its sides. I suspected it was the same truck that would have been sent if I had been willing to pay 85 pounds for the visit. Within five minutes the tire was changed and our luggage restored into the boot. I'll bet Arnold Clarke did not have to pay $150 for this service. My only concern was that for the rest of our trip, I would not have a spare tire. I confess, that thought was a little disconcerting.

The city of Edinburgh is built out from the base of Edinburgh Castle, the most famous of Scottish castles. It is in this castle that Mary Queen of Scots gave birth to James the VI of Scotland, who later became James I of England. Within this castle, the Crown Jewels of Scotland are stored, as is the Coronation Stone on which Scottish Kings were crowned. From the castle walls, one looks out over and beyond the modern city of Edinburgh and, like all great cities, one can scarcely glimpse it in one day. The castle, itself, hosts several museums dedicated to the history of Scottish military units. It also has the obligatory memorial to those who died during the Great War, 1914-1918; the war that changed the face of Europe. Unless one reads a great deal of history, one cannot comprehend the tragedy of World War I, particularly for Great Britain. Not only was the flower of its manhood lost but also the world to which the survivors returned was not the world from which the left, and would never be so again. No matter where Jane and I have traveled in England, Scotland, and Wales, we see in the smallest churches in the smallest villages memorials and remembrances to those who were killed in that war. In Edinburgh, as in London, Manchester, Glasgow, or Dornoch, one can witness the creativity of humankind in art and architecture and be reminded of the destruction of humankind in war museums and memorials.

With our one-day visit to Edinburgh a limiting factor, Jane and I concentrated our wanderings to exploring the Royal Mile, the main thoroughfare of medieval Edinburgh, linking Edinburgh Castle on one end to the Holyrood Palace on the other. In between is the Scotch Whiskey Centre, the Tollbooth Kirk, with the city's highest spire, St. Giles Cathedral from which John Knox directed the Scottish Reformation and in which is a carved royal pew used by the Queen when she stays in Edinburgh. In Scotland, she is not Head of the Church, as she is in England; she is simply a member of the Church of Scotland. Since it was nearing Halloween, and if we had had the time and inclination, we could have taken a tour of the haunted underground vaults of the city and heard tales of torture, hauntings, and witchcraft. Alas, we only had time for the living; or the living history in Parliament House, built in 1639 and the City Chambers, designed in the 1750s. At the end of the Royal Mile is the Palace of Holyroodhouse, the Queen's official residence when she is in Scotland. This palace was the home of Mary, Queen of Scots and it was here that her husband, Lord Darnley, was murdered by her Italian secretary, David Rizzio. It was from here that she fled to England, where she was held prisoner for twenty years by Elizabeth I, before being charged with treason and executed. The Palace is open to the public, unless the present Queen is in residence.

Midway along the Royal Mile, Jane and I found a tearoom in which to rest, have some tea, a blueberry muffin, and a visit to the facilities. (We seemed to be the only customers without either a laptop computer opened in front of us or a cell phone adhesived to our ear.) Thus reinforced, we continued in wonder as we wandered. Our only detour from the Royal Mile was a brief visit to the Edinburgh railway station. We love European trains and train stations. With the exception of Grand Central Station in New York, America's great train stations have been either torn down or converted into combination train stations and shopping malls. We love the hustle and bustle of train stations and like to stand under the great destination boards to watch the flashing of times for arrivals and departures. Trains are a wonderfully civilized way to travel if one wants to see the countryside through which one is traveling. Jane and I and our daughter once took the train from Zurich to Geneva on Christmas Day and watched as many of our fellow travelers, laden with presents, exited into the small villages along the way to spend that day with family. It was great fun.

At about 4:30pm, we decided that we had better try to find our way out of the city and toward the village of Gullane, where we were to spend the night in the Faussethill Guesthouse. This distance was not far but, from the center of Edinburgh, I was not sure of the direction. I knew, of course, that I had to go East, but from the center of town, which way was East? I reasoned that if I drove toward the setting sun, I would know that we were going in the wrong direction. On our walk back toward the car park, we saw a sign with the number of our road on it. I took this to be a sign and, with Jane as navigator, followed it. Somewhere along the way, trying to keep abreast of bus only lanes, turn only lanes, and no turn lanes, while keeping my place in the queue with thousands of others streaming out of the city at this time of the day, we lost our sign. I found a small petrol station, which was, fortunately, on my side of the road and stopped to ask for directions. I would have been too proud to do that in the U.S. but here, no one knew me so I was confident the word would not get spread about. Asking was, of course, Jane's suggestion to which I simply acquiesced. We had, indeed, missed our turn but, if we continued in the direction in which we were going we would come to the Ring road that encircled the city and by turning to the left we would once again find ourselves heading in the direction in which we wished to go. It was as had been foretold and we soon left Edinburgh behind us. I knew that Gullane was not too distant from Edinburgh but, as I saw the sign to exit whiz by me, I realized that it was not quite as far as I had remembered. Since we were on a motorway, we had to drive another five miles before we found an exit that would allow us to cross over the motorway and retrace our route. This time, we exited where we were supposed to and quickly found ourselves in the village of Gullane.

Faussethill Guesthouse is the home of George and Dorothy Nixon. I had stayed in their lovely home on a previous occasion and knew that Jane and I would be very comfortable. It had been a tiring day and the drive from the center of Edinburgh had not been without stress. A cup of tea in their comfortable second floor sitting room looking out over their well-tended yard was a delightful respite from the day's activities that had begun in St. Andrews, continued through the attractions of the Royal Mile in Edinburgh, and now would end in the lovely golfing area of Gullane.

East Lothian is not the biggest county in this part of Scotland, but within its limited area it boasts a number of the finest collection of golf courses in the country. The best known of these is Muirfield, home to the Honourable Company of Edinburgh Golfers, arguably the oldest golf club in the world with records that date back to 1744. I had wanted to play Muirfield on this trip but, as a single golfer, I could not get a tee time. The Honourable Company of Edinburgh Golfers restricts their non-member tee times to two ball and four ball only. But Muirfield is only one of a multitude of golf courses in the immediate area. Gullane (No. 1), where I was scheduled to play the next day, North Berwick, where I had previously played in the wind and rain, Dunbar, Whitekirk and Luffness are wonderful and memorable venues. Gifford, with its picturesque holes, is always a delight. Royal Musselburgh and Longneddry offer an alternative to links golf and the Old Course within the racetrack at Musselburgh (the oldest race course in Scotland) is one of the original Open Championship courses. Golfers, if they wished, could simply check into the Faussethill Guesthouse for a week and enjoy seven memorable days of golf on seven, or ten, or twelve challenging and memorable golf courses. So many golf courses. So little time.

After dark, Jane and I wandered down the High Street of Gullane to the Golf Inn, a small hotel with an intimate dining room. We were shown to a snug corner were we relaxed and revisited the day over drinks, soup, lemon sole, wine, and coffee. These leisurely evenings in small hotel dining rooms are wonderful ways to end hectic days of driving and sightseeing. We stretched the evening because my tee time for the next morning was not until 10:30am. We knew we could enjoy an unhurried morning tomorrow.

As we approached our guesthouse, we noticed a taxi at the curb and four men standing at the front door. We soon learned that four more American golfers had joined our company. As it turned out, this brief encounter at the door was the only time we were to see them. They were leaving immediately for dinner at Greywalls, a wonderful old hotel built in 1901 overlooking Muirfield Golf Club. We greeted them, said goodnight to our hosts, went to our room, found some quiet music on the radio, and drifted into sleep. Our sixth day had proved to be as unpredictable as the others and we would not have had it any other way.

Day Seven

Day seven dawned clear and windy. We wandered down to breakfast at 8:30am. Dorothy Nixon appeared with coffee and asked what we wanted for breakfast. Poached eggs, bacon, toast, and marmalade were soon placed before us. We commented on the clearness of the day and that we were able to see Bass Rock from our bedroom window. Dorothy told us that, if we had the time, a visit to the Scottish Seabird Centre in North Berwick was worth the trip. Interactive cameras were now placed all over Bass Rock and visitors at the Centre could view up close the renowned seabird colonies on the rock. Our schedule would not permit that visit on this trip. We asked about the other guests. Dorothy smiled and just shook her head. With a little prompting, we learned that the four men we had met briefly the night before were, like us, on a golfing trip but, unlike us, they were traveling from golf course to golf course by taxi. They had come to Gullane the night before from Edinburgh by taxi. They had an early tee time at Muirfield and had asked the Nixons if they would call for a taxi. George explained that Gullane was a small village and did not have taxi service. How were they to get to Muirfield, they asked? The only solution was for George to take them in his car. George has a very small car, which not only required him to make two trips to Muirfield but also necessitated that the men riding in the back seat of the car stack their golf clubs on their laps. They had left an inordinate amount of luggage in the back room of the guesthouse. Dorothy told us that they were going from Gullane to Turnberry on the southern coast. I gasped. That was over a hundred miles. From Turnberry, they were going to Carnoustie. I couldn't believe it. That would be a trip of over one hundred and fifty miles from Turnberry back in the direction from which they had come. Had they even looked at a map of Scotland before they planned their trip? They had obviously made no arrangements for transportation other than calling taxis. Jane offered the opinion that they had more money than sense. I could not conceive of such an arrangement. I am sure that they had a great trip but I expect their transportation expenses cost more than their golf. I am confident they made some taxi drivers very, very happy.

The weather was so extraordinary for this time of the year, Jane and I commented on it again. Dorothy said that because of the unusually warm summer, she and George had had guests seven days a week since March. Business was great but they had not had a day to themselves. In November, she said, they were closing the house and heading to Majorca for a few weeks. Jane and I reasoned that they had earned it.

Although the golf course was only a few blocks away, Jane and I have learned that B&B hosts like their guests to be away early so that they can begin to prepare for the next arrivals. We said our goodbyes to

George and Dorothy and drove to the Gullane Golf Club.

Golf has been played on the Gullane Links for over 300 years and the Gullane Golf Club was established in 1882. There are three beautiful courses at this club which, over the years, has hosted a number of championships. The American golfer "Babe" Zaharias won the British Ladies Championship here in 1947. In 2004, the British Ladies Open Amateur Championship was played on these courses. There is a visitor's clubhouse which has been open for about ten years but, since I was scheduled to play Gullane No. 1, which "is one of the final qualifying courses for the Open Championship when it is played at Muirfield," I had access to the members clubhouse, a large white building across the road from the first tee of Gullane No. 1. I check in at the reception desk, was given my badge, then Jane and I walked across the road to drop my golf bag at the first tee, then go to the member's clubhouse for coffee. There was a two day old *USA Today* lying on a table so we were able to catch up on US news not carried by the BBC evening radio broadcasts. At 10:25am I reported to the lst tee for my 10:30am tee time. A fourball of women was teeing off as we arrived. The starter told me that I would be playing alone, (again) which was fine with Jane and me because it allowed me to play at my leisure and allowed Jane to search the rough for golf balls (of which she found one all week) and to take photographs of anything that caught her eye.

This day was a great day to both play golf and take photographs at Gullane No. 1. Although it was windy, the sky was clear and what a clear sky means at Gullane No. 1 is that one can see for miles. The course is not a flat, seaside course. It is a hilly seaside course winding up, down, and around Gullane Hill. The first hole is a relatively short par 4, and the second is a tough par 4 up a gradual incline. The first green is protected on three sides by slopes covered with heavy, heather-like grasses. I hit my second shot five feet to the left of the green and never found my ball. I didn't even find someone else's ball. The grasses are so heavy and matted that looking for a ball that flies into them is usually a hopeless task.

True to its reputation, the view from the 7th tee of Gullane No. 1 is truly spectacular. At the highest point on the course, one looks out from this tee at the Firth of Forth. On this particular morning, there were large cargo ships plying its waters. From this teeing area one also looks down on Muirfield, home of the Honourable Company of Edinburgh Golfers, where our guesthouse mates were presently playing. Try as we might, photographs, even panoramic ones, could not capture for posterity the beauty offered us in all directions from this teeing area. From the golfer's point of view, however, the tee shot is downhill.

Teeing area, 7th Hole, Gullane #1 Course

**Barriers to repel tanks: World War II, Gullane #1
Course**

Playing a fairway parallel to the coast, Jane and I noticed a number of large, concrete squares along the edge of the fairway. We wondered what they were, since, upon closer inspection, they seemed to line the entire edge of the golf course. We saw two men rebuilding the sod face of a bunker and asked about the concrete. They told us that these huge blocks were put in place during World War II to prevent tanks from landing along this coastline. Since this was the East Coast of Scotland, facing Europe across the channel, this made a great deal of sense to us. I hoped that a golfer could get relief if one's golf ball found itself behind one of these objects. The loose impediment rule did not seem to apply to this circumstance.

This is truly a course worth playing but, I imagined, that in the wind and the rain, this would be a demanding and an exacting golf course. On the day I played it, one of the par 5 holes played directly into the wind and I thought that I would never find the green. The 17th teeing area, from the top of a hill, offers a view facing away from the Firth of Forth toward the village of Gullane and the golf course clubhouse down below. Beyond the clubhouse, Gullane No. 2 and Gullane No. 3 courses can be seen almost in their entirety. The numbering of the courses should not mislead the golfer. No. 2 has also been used as a final qualifying course for the Open and No. 3, though shorter than the others, is as challenging a test as any golfer would want. I thoroughly enjoyed my round of golf in this beautiful environment, and Jane enjoyed the exercise and the vistas.

Over coffee in the clubhouse, we checked our map and planned our drive to our final destination on this trip; the lovely golfing town of Troon southwest of Glasgow. We planned to spend the next three nights in Troon before checking into a hotel at the Glasgow airport on the final night of this holiday.

The quickest way for us to have driven from Gullane to Troon would have been to take the M8 to Glasgow then the A77 to Troon. This holiday, however, was not about speed but about leisure. We chose the A71 south from Edinburgh which would take us through the center of the lowlands, keep us well south of Glasgow, and bring us into Troon from the east. It would be about a 93 mile drive and we allowed for three hours to make this drive through the countryside. We pointed our compass toward Kilmarnock and headed southwest. It was as we had hoped; a narrow road, small farms and villages, sheep grazing in the fields, and a bright sunny afternoon. Everything was going smoothly until we got to Larkhall. As we exited a roundabout on the A71, we suddenly found our road barricaded. ROAD CLOSED. I pulled to the side of the road. I knew we would not get lost but I didn't know how far I would have to go north in order to find another main road that went west. I noticed that there was a police car parked at the barricade. As I got out of my car, he started to pull away. I shouted and began to run after him. Fortunately, he saw me and stopped.

"I am a tourist attempting to get to Troon on the A71," I explained.

"Follow me," he said.

If Jane and I thought that the A71 was a narrow road, we were in for a surprise. For the next ten minutes, the neighborhood police constable led us down lanes shadowed by overhanging trees; between stone walls that we could have touch by stretching our arm out of the car window; with lay-bys to pull into to let approaching traffic pass or for them to let us pass; and as winding as the walking paths they must have been one hundred years ago. To keep up with our guide, I drove at least twenty miles an hour faster than I would have had I been on my own. After several sharp twists and turns and two turns to the right, we found ourselves at the edge of a small town. The policeman pulled his car to the side of the road and walked back toward us.

"At the top of the hill, turn left and you will be back on the A71."

We both thanked him profusely. We wondered where we might have wandered without his assistance. My experience with the constabulary of Great Britain has been limited, for the most part, to asking directions; although in 1985, when I was a visiting professor at the University of Manchester, I had to register at the Didsbury Village police station as an 'alien'. ("Beam me up, Scotty.") I recalled to Jane my first visit to London many years ago. Walking out of Victoria Station, I asked a London Bobby if he could tell me how to get to Buckingham Palace. "Walk straight down this street," he said. "It's the last big house on the left."

Once again on a road that was on a map we felt comfortable and confident that we would ultimately arrive where we had intended. When I saw a sign

91

directing us to Prestwick Airport, I knew that we were close.

The Copper Beech Guesthouse in Troon is the home of George and Norma McLardy. It is a large stone house with a walled yard and garden. Many of the houses on this quiet street that leads to the Royal Troon Golf Links are behind large walls. I had stayed at the Copper Beech before. I pulled through the gate and onto the gravel parking area. I am always glad to get to where I am going. I began pulling bags from the car while Jane rang the door bell. No answer. Not what I wanted at the end of a long drive.

I walked around the house. No one was in sight. Oh, well. We will just sit here and wait. Presently, from the greenhouse at the edge of the yard, a man appeared with some keys. It was not George McLardy.

Copper Beech Guest House, Home of George and Norma McLardy

"I will let you in and show you to your room," he told us. "The McLardy's will be here shortly."

We put our bags in the room, washed our faces, and wandered down stairs to the sitting room to relax. Within minutes I heard a car on the gravel and looking from the sitting room window, recognized my hosts. I went to the door to let them in.

"I'm sorry," I said as I opened the door. "We have no vacancies."

George laughed. Norma looked puzzled.

George McLardy is a gregarious man. He never meets a stranger and he is a thoughtful host. A heart attack a number of years ago encouraged him to turn his attractive home into a bed and breakfast. Within walking distance of the Royal Troon Golf Links, it is an ideal location to take in guests and for the guests it is a wonderful respite from hotels. George has never traveled far from Glasgow, yet he has seen the world through the guests he hosts in his home. His speech is heavy with the sound of his native tongue and one often misses a word or two because of his accent. I would judge him to be in his middle to late fifties, perhaps sixty. He and Norma came into the sitting room to greet Jane then Norma retired to the private quarters of the house while George made himself comfortable with us in the sitting room.

"How about a glass of sherry?" he asked.

We assented immediately. George is a teller of stories. Not all of them are politically correct but, hey, it is his house. He told us that since I had last been there, Dan and Marilyn Quayle, the former U.S. Vice

President and his wife, had stayed there. He said that Dan was quiet and on a schedule but that Marilyn was open and friendly; interested and interesting. She had come to find the grave of her great grandfather. George told us that, with a little research, he had been able to find where her great grandfather had been buried. He encouraged her to visit the grave. "I assured her that her great grandfather would be in to receive visitors," he told us. The last time the Open had been played at Royal Troon, George had leased his whole house to Seve Ballesteros' father-in-law. When Seve came to visit George asked, "And whom shall I say is calling?" George told us over sherry that his latest venture was buying himself a motorcycle. He was taking lessons on how to ride it so that he could drive about the countryside in his powder blue leathers. Norma begged him not to pull up anywhere where she and her friends were having lunch. I suspected that George would like nothing better.

Jane and I had not eaten since our late breakfast at the Faussethill Guesthouse, hours and miles earlier. The Piersland House Hotel is but a short walk from the Copper Beech. Piersland House is an old-world looking hotel across the road from the Portland Course of the Royal Troon Golf Club. I like this hotel because it has a formal dining room and an informal dining room. Jane and I opted for the informal room and spent a leisurely hour and a half over drinks and dinner. We speculated that all of the tables inhabited only with men were golfers. We were so comfortable that we decided a cognac would be a nice treat and a wonderful way to extend the evening. We were glad we had warm coats for the walk back to Copper Beech. The down comforter on the bed was the last thing of which I was aware as the seventh day came to a close.

Day Eight

George McLardy has a collection of miniature flags of the world's countries. He has a centerpiece for the dining table in which he displays the flag of the country of his guests and, if he has one, in the case of guests from the U.S., their state flag. Jane and I were the only guests at Copper Beech on this morning and when we came down to breakfast, the American flag was prominently displayed on the table. I had wanted to bring George a small flag of the State of Georgia to add to his collection but since our state has recently changed its flag, I could not find a small one to bring. Since the times during when I had previously stayed here, unless my memory was faulty, George had taken to wearing a white chef's jacket when serving breakfast. On this morning, as I had a tee time at Turnberry for 10:06am, Jane and I had plenty of time for a quiet breakfast alone in the dining room. George wandered in and out, bringing coffee and more toast and asking us about our plans for the day. He wanted to know if I knew the best way to drive to Turnberry and proceeded to draw me a map on the back of a piece of paper. As it happened, his map was exactly the route I would have followed. As the crow flies, it is not far in miles between Troon and Turnberry. Since we would be driving and not flying, however, I allowed for an hour to drive the approximately thirty miles. The A77 would take us through Prestwick, Maybole, and Kirkoswald. Maybole was larger than I had anticipated and the early morning traffic confirmed the wisdom of our decision to leave early. Beyond Maybole, we were immediately in the countryside. We passed a small, stone abbey and marked its location so that we could visit it upon our return, if we came back this way. Unfortunately, we did not get back to it. We continued to be blessed with unseasonably warm and clear weather. The drive was lovely.

Upon seeing Turnberry Resort for the first time, Jane and I immediately compared it to the Greenbrier Resort in West Virginia, substituting the ocean for the mountains. The hotel is large, it is white, it is elegant and, it is expensive. We considered spending one night there but, since Troon was so close, we decided that the packing, unpacking, and additional expense was not worth the effort for just one night.

We arrived early and, after presenting myself in the pro shop, Jane and I had time to purchase a few items then sit, with coffee, in the lounge overlooking the putting green. My tee time, as it turned out, could be established earlier than had been previously scheduled; to 9:30am. We decided to take advantage of the extra half and hour and at 9:20am, we presented ourselves to the starter on the Ailsa Course.

"Mr. Coomer, the party you were to play with has cancelled. You will be playing alone."

I was beginning to think that word of my golf game had seeped out throughout the country and that golfers were calling starters at golf courses to insure that they were not going to be forced to play with me. For Jane and me, however, it was to be another leisurely round of golf with me playing against the course and against myself; a formidable foe.

Teeing area, 9th Hole, Turnberry Ailsa Course

Ailsa Course, Turnberry Resort

"Would you like for me to take your picture?" asked the starter. Jane handed him our camera and we posed with the imposing hotel as a backdrop. He watched with an experienced eye as I hit my first tee shot. He nodded slightly towards me as my ball found the fairway. I suspected that he could write an interesting book entitled "Tee Shots I Have Seen." We were off.

Turnberry has a fascinating history that is well worth reading. Suffice it to say in these pages that in both World Wars of the 20th century, the course was used as an air base. During the Second World War, the hotel was used as a military hospital and concrete runways were poured to handle heavy aircraft takeoffs and landings. After WWII, few expected golf to be played on these seaside links again. In the late 1940s, the British government allocated some money to Turnberry as compensation for its wartime use. In 1951, the new Ailsa course was opened and by 1957,

Turnberry was again hosting PGA events. In 1987, the resort became part of the Nitto Kogyo Corporation of Japan which invested 25 million pounds in refurbishing the hotel and modernizing the maintenance and irrigation system for the golf courses. A modern clubhouse was also built. Today, Turnberry is as elegant a resort as it must have been 100 years ago when Edwardian guests arrived by rail directly to the back entrances of the hotel.

Jane and I have been fortunate to visit some lovely hotels in the U.S. and Europe. Turnberry ranks among the loveliest, both in its setting and in its ambiance.

On the third hole of the Ailsa course, Jane and I caught up with a four ball. It was two women and two young boys. They graciously waved for me to play through. One of the hardest things in golf is to keep one's concentration when being allowed to play through another group of golfers. The tendency is to hurry so as to move on out of the way. I drove the ball beyond where the foursome was waiting for me. Under their watchful eye, I hit a seven wood into the greenside bunker but was able to get up and down for a par. Waving my appreciation for their courtesy, I moved toward the next tee. We did not see them again the rest of the round. In keeping with the rest of the week, the weather was benign which allowed me to enjoy both the beauty and the challenge of this golf course. Holes four through twelve follow the coastline and on this day, the views out over the Irish Sea were spectacular. The Ailsa Craig, for which this course is named and the Island of Arran, for which the companion course at

Turnberry was formally named, (the second course was altered several years ago and is now called the Kintyre Course which is used as a qualifying course for the Open Championship) stood out as though they were large, dark silhouettes against the blue sky and water.

In my experience, I have always selected the tee shot at the eighteenth hole at Pebble Beach as the most spectacular and daunting of any I had every played. When I got to the ninth tee at Turnberry's Ailsa course, however, I changed my mind. Since Jane and I were alone, I walked down to the championship teeing area on the ninth hole. This teeing area is built on a rocky ledge extending out over the waves crashing in on the rocks below. One cannot see the green from the tee. The target from the teeing area is a stone cairn that marks the fairway and the drive must carry over two hundred yards of cliffs and surf to reach it. Fortunately, I was able to play my second shot with the same ball that I hit from the tee. To add to the beauty of this golf hole, a lighthouse sits on a promontory to the left of the fairway. To add to its history, the remains of the castle of Robert the Bruce (1272) can be seen from the ninth green. This is, truly, one of the great golf holes in the world. A Scottish friend told me that, a number of years ago there was a well known British golfer who suffered from vertigo. When he played this hole, his caddie had to blindfold him, lead him down to the teeing area where the golfer would take off the blindfold, hit his tee shot, replace the blindfold, and be led by his caddie back to the fairway. It is a story easily believed.

On both the fifteenth and sixteenth holes, I learned that ignorance is bliss. The fifteenth hole is a par 3, aptly named Ca' Canny (Take Care). From the medal tees, from where I was playing, it was about 170 yards. It looked like a straightforward par 3. I hit a six iron and my ball landed on the front right of the green. As Jane and I walked toward the green, we saw the ground fall away into rough covered hollows and when we got to the green I saw that there was a severe drop from the right of the green of about fifteen feet into deep rough. Had I known what this hole really looked like when I was on the teeing area, I would not have been so cavalier about my shot. The name of the next hole, the sixteenth, should have warned me: Wee Burn. Wilson's Burn runs directly in front of the elevated green. It cannot be seen from the fairway. Under clubbing one's second shot may mean a wet ball, though not a lost ball, since the Burn is only about three feet wide and three inches deep. It is there, however, and must be guarded against.

The eighteenth hole is a straightforward, 400-yard par 4 and it plays directly toward the hotel, which is always, from this fairway, impressively, in one's sight. For those staying there, it signals a welcome for the comfort that is to come. Jane and I reserved this comfort for another time.

After placing my golf clubs in the car and changing my shoes, Jane and I returned to the lounge in the clubhouse to lunch on soup, bread, and cheese and to plan our afternoon, or rather, to confirm previously made plans for the afternoon.

Culzean (pronounced Cullain) Castle is about a ten-minute drive from Turnberry. Its historical foundations date to the 16th century. Its more recent restoration dates from the 1970s. It was from within this castle that General Dwight Eisenhower worked during the Second World War and, in gratitude for his efforts, the top floor of Culzean Castle was given to him as a gift through his lifetime. That floor is not now open to the public but it contains several large apartments that can be rented as private accommodations. I confess that Jane and I did not even give a passing thought to making this lovely castle our base while in the area. We did, however, enjoy the pleasure of wandering the lovely rooms inside and the magnificent gardens outside on a sunny afternoon. The office from which Eisenhower worked can be viewed but, aside from historical interest, it detracts from the restored 18th century ambiance of the castle with its elegant furnishings. The parlor, built to the edge of the cliffs, offers an unobstructed view of the Firth of Clyde. On this clear day we could not only see the Island of Arran and the Ailsa Craig, but also we could glimpse Northern Island on the horizon. I wondered if those who lived on this site over the years ever tired of the view. It would, of course, change with the weather but it would be in the changing, at least for me, that would keep the view ever new.

Like many European castles that gradually became country homes, Culzean Castle is nestled in a park environment. The grounds of the castle became Scotland's first public country park in 1969 and the gardens and walkways, the fountain court and the swan pond, the deer park and the walled garden, afford the visitor hours of pleasurable exploration. The walled garden, fruit trees, flowers, herbs, and fir trees protected from the wind by a twelve-foot stonewall, is a quiet oasis in which to take a relaxing stroll. Jane and I enjoy wandering European gardens from end to end. We have, on occasion, lost track of time. Once while we were taking a late afternoon stroll in the gardens of Hever Castle, the childhood home of Anne Bolen, we noted how quiet and peaceful it was. It seemed as though we were the only two there. As it turned out, we were. When we returned to the entry gate, we found that we were locked in. The wooden doors were fifteen feet high and secured with a large beam. The walls were too high to climb. We could not find a security person. We faced the prospect of being locked in Hever Castle for the night. In studying our dilemma, we noticed that although the heavy wooden doors were secure, the beam could be shifted and the metal rods resting in the ground could be lifted. After one last effort to find a caretaker, I lifted the beam, Jane freed the rods from the ground and we opened the giant doors only enough to extract ourselves from our temporary confinement. We pushed the doors closed behind us and beat a quick retreat to our car. Anne Bolen should have been so lucky.

On this day, however, we exited in a timely fashion from Culzean and, consulting our map, discovered that we could take a different route back to Troon from the one by which we had come. The wonderful thing about this day's adventures is that they had taken place within a twenty-five minute drive of the Copper Beech. We were back early enough in the evening for a glass of sherry with George McLardy and to recite our day's activities.

The Reverend Alastair H. Symington, MA, BD, Chaplain to Her Majesty the Queen in Scotland, and pastor of the Troon Old Parish Church lives two blocks from our guesthouse in Bentinck Drive in Troon. Alastair has preached in our church in Atlanta and I had previously visited with him and his wife, Eileen in their home in Troon. When I wrote to him that Jane and I were coming to Troon, he graciously invited us to dinner in their home. Alastair has several things in his life that could stir the sin of envy in others. He has a lovely wife and two daughters. He is pastor of a beautiful old church. He is occasionally called upon by the British Royal family for advice and he lives within walking distance of the entrance to the Royal Troon Golf Club. But what rouses the sin of envy in me is that he has a son-in-law who is a golf professional which, I assume, means free golf lessons. Among his other attributes, Alastair is a golfer. When he was last in Atlanta, he had the opportunity to play golf at Augusta National and he has the video to prove it. Our pre-dinner conversation kept coming back to the courses that I had played on this trip and what else we had been doing. He said that his Friday morning was open and asked if I would like to play his club; the Glasgow Golf Club. I deferred to Jane because we had decided that Friday, our last day in Scotland, would be a tourist day. Jane encouraged me to play, saying that she would spend the morning walking along the beach in Troon and wandering about its central area. Eileen reminded Alastair that they had to drive to visit their daughter and that they must be there by 1:00pm. Alastair, golfer that he is, reasoned that if he and I could get the first tee time, about 8:00am, we could finish in time for him to meet his schedule. I, having been a party to many a golfer, golfer's wife conversation, sensed a lack of enthusiasm for this arrangement on the part of the golfer's wife. I said that I did not want to jeopardize a previous commitment on his part but Alastair felt that if he picked me up at 7:40am, we could play a quick round and be back by 11:00am. I again deferred to Jane who, knowing that I would like to play another course that I had not previously played, insisted that she would like an unscheduled free morning on her own. I knew that Jane did not want to walk another golf course this week but I also knew that she would enjoy a morning of leisure. Alastair and I set a date for Friday.

Dinner in the home of acquaintances, particularly in another country, is always enjoyable. We did not talk about golf at dinner. We talked about family (our daughter had recently married, one of their daughters was about to marry), we talked about mutual friends in Atlanta, we talked about politics (the war in Iraq and the relatively new Scottish parliament), and we talked about theology (Alastair from a position of vocation, me from a position of avocation.) Good food, good wine, good company; it was a delightful end to a delightful day. Jane and I walked the two blocks to

Copper Beech in the cold October night. It had been another full day. We would never have done this much in one day had we been home but, hey, we were on holiday. It was the morning and the evening of the eighth day.

Day Nine

When planning this trip, I had to decide which of two courses in the area Jane would most enjoy walking and seeing; Royal Troon, scene of the upcoming Open in 2004, or Prestwick, the site of the first Open in 1860. Although both courses are not in Troon, their boundaries meet in such a way that it is possible to play the outgoing nine holes of Royal Troon, cross the boundary and play the incoming nine holes at Prestwick. After lunch, an energetic foursome could then play the outgoing nine holes of Prestwick, cross the boundary and play the incoming nine holes at Royal Troon. I do not know if this is presently possible but I have read that it was not an uncommon occurrence in the past. Royal Troon is a beautiful seaside links course, with its picturesque par-3, 126 yard Postage Stamp on which 71 year old Gene Sarazen scored an ace. Prestwick, on the other hand, is unique; beginning with its first hole paralleling the railroad track that can, and has, contributed to a fortuitous bounce of the ball off of the side of a moving train. An ancient churchyard sits opposite the first green.

I decided that I would like for Jane to see the historic Prestwick Golf Club, originally laid out in twelve holes by Old Tom Morris. As a single, my tee time was scheduled for 7:50am. Needless to say, George McLardy was not overly enthused by this early demand on his time. Jane and I said we would be content with a cold breakfast but George insisted on a full Scottish breakfast to stoke up our furnaces for a chilly October morning.

**First hole at Prestwick Golf Club, with Railroad Station
(and tracks to left) and Clubhouse in center**

I knew that Prestwick was but a short drive from Troon but we left at 7:15am to avoid any problems with time. We arrived in the parking lot of the Prestwick Golf Club at 7:25am. It was pitch dark. We longed for a local McDonalds where we could get a cup of coffee. We sat in the car waiting for the dawn. Within a few minutes, another car arrived. "Ah, another early morning golfer," I thought. A car door opened and out bounded a man and his dog; not a golfer, just a man bringing his dog to the course for a morning run. I confess, it was rather enjoyable sitting there watching daily life begin in and around Prestwick. About 7:45am, we saw a light in the lobby of the clubhouse. I put on my golf shoes, picked up my bag and we headed for the warmth of that brownstone building.

"Mr. Coomer?" inquired the porter. "I am afraid that you will be playing alone this morning."

Jane's look said, "Why should this be a surprise?" As she headed for the women's locker room, she paused at the bar to inquire if, perhaps, they had some coffee. It was, I am afraid, a little early for amenities. The porter handed me a course guide and a scorecard. Although I was the only golfer within sight, I knew to wait until precisely 7:50 before teeing my ball. I went to the area of the first tee to limber up. At the train station adjacent to the first tee, several people were standing on the platform waiting for a morning train in Glasgow. They looked at me as though I was just another normal sight at this time of the morning. Jane brought me the news that I could "play away," the porter deciding that he would rather send the news instead of delivering it in person, which would require that he leave his warm desk inside the clubhouse. I teed it up, selected a seven wood and, under the watchful eye of my gallery at the train station, hit the ball out into the fairway. I was greatly relieved that I did not slice it directly into the path of the oncoming commuter train.

The Prestwick Golf Course requires what many golfers refer to as "target" golf, meaning that shots must be played toward areas on most holes in order to enhance the following shot. Few holes at Prestwick allow for a driver from the teeing area, including the first hole where a middle iron or a seven wood is encouraged in order to place the ball in play between the stone wall separating the railroad tracks from the fairway on the right side and the buckthorn bushes and rough on the left. The third hole, with its famous Cardinal Bunker, requires either prior experience or the assistance of a caddie on the second shot because the line to the fairway and toward the green is not obvious. On the fifth tee, a 206 yard, par-3 hole named "Himalayas," Jane, looking around, asked, "Where is the green?"

I replied, "Do you see those three colored disks on the side of that hill directly in front of us? The middle one is my target. I have to hit the ball over 'the Himalayas' and the green is in that direction." I knew that I could hit my seven wood over "the Himalayas" but I could not hit it both high enough and far enough to reach the green. Oh, well, first things first. I hit it high enough, but not long enough.

On two previous occasions when playing this historic course, I had had a caddie who would suggest a line of ball flight from the teeing area. On one's own, selecting a direction for ball flight could be hazardous to one's score. I explored an inordinate number of bunkers on this early morning round at Prestwick. It is, indeed, a unique golf course and it is not difficult to imagine Old Tom and Young Tom Morris, in their woolen plus fours, with their wooden clubs and gutta-percha golf balls, winning the early Open Championships over these grounds.

From the 18th tee, I remembered the advice of my caddie from a previous trip: aim for the clock on the face of the clubhouse. Although the line is well to the left of the green, the slope of the fairway, if the ball is hit along that line, will move the ball toward the green. The hole is a short, 284 yard, par 4, and it is possible to drive this green with a three wood. I didn't expect to reach the green with a three wood this morning but I thought a good drive would put me in the area in front of the green where I would have a short pitch shot into the green. As it turned out, that is what happened and I two putted for a par. It was only 11:00am. I changed into my street shoes and we headed into the clubhouse for some hot coffee.

With the whole of the afternoon free, Jane and I headed to Alloway to visit the cottage where the poet, Robert Burns, was born and lived during the early part of his life. Although he spent little of his life in this small village, there is a huge monument to him here and his famous story, *Tam o'Shanter,* is said to have been set in Alloway. We had been told that there was a quaint hotel in Alloway called Brig o'Doon Hotel, which served wonderful meals. We decided to have a late lunch and had little difficulty finding this small hotel. Since we had not previously booked, we could not get a table by the large window with a view of Brig o"Doon (Bridge over the Doon River) but we had a delightful lunch of soup, salad, and wine in the cozy confines of this small dining room. It is obviously a popular place. We observed small groups of well dressed women lunching together and several groups of elderly couples, dressed for a luncheon outing, enjoying the hospitality of this hotel. Jane and I were glad we were seated against a wall, since our casual dress was not so noticeable. After our lunch, we walked to the beautiful, arched brown stone bridge which lent its name to the hotel. I could almost see Cyd Charisse waiting for Gene Kelly to come running back over this bridge to her and the mystical life of Brigadoon. The river and the gardens of the Brig o'Doon Hotel offered the opportunity for some beautiful photographs. It is an enchanting setting.

The Burns Cottage, though modernized for visitors, contains some of the original furniture from the time that Robert Burn's father built the cottage in the 1750s. There is simplicity about this place that is attractive. The original living area conveys the feeling of overcrowding and lack of any privacy. As opposed to the castles we had visited, this was the manner in which most people of the day lived. The museum, next to the cottage is basically two large rooms cluttered with Robert Burns memorabilia, including the ubiquitous pictures of royal visits over the years. The late Princess Margaret is pictured during a visit as well as the Queen, Elizabeth, during a dedication. Burn's poem, *Tam o'Shanter* is featured in pictures and in models of scenes from the story. In a separate building, one can walk through a recreation of the story. Jane and I opted to walk about the village. Our trek to the Burns cottage reminded Jane of a trip we had made to visit the isolated vicarage in which the Bronte sisters had grown up in Howarth, England. We were glad to have made the effort but it did not remain high on a list of places to revisit.

Early evening found us back at Copper Beech, in the lounge with George, reminiscing about our day over a glass of sherry. I had to break the news to George that I would need an early breakfast again the next morning since I would be picked up at 7:45am. Europeans are late risers and I knew George wished that I were a later riser who scheduled his golf at a more reasonable time of day. We were his guests, however, and he wished to accommodate us. Since we were the only guests at this time, it was much easier to do.

As we had done on Tuesday evening, Jane and I walked to the Piersland Hotel for dinner. There was a larger crowd in the informal dining area but we were able to get the last empty table for two. We stretched our dinner into two comfortable hours then walked back through the quiet streets of Troon for our last night at Copper Beech.

Day Ten

The Reverend Alastair Symington pulled into the Copper Beech parking area right on time; 7:45am. Jane and I had packed the night before and I had already brought our baggage down to the lounge so that George McLardy could begin to prepare the rooms for his next guests. Jane was going to spend the morning reading, followed by a walk along the beach to the High Street in Troon. Alastair and I were going to have a quick round of golf at his club, the Glasgow Golf Club, Gailes Links. I was wearing a jacket and a tie. Like nearly all European private clubs, the Glasgow Golf Club requires that men must wear a coat and tie when entering the clubhouse. We would change into our golf clothes in the club's locker room. We were not, as it turned out, the first to arrive. There were four other men chatting and changing into golf togs in the locker room. Alastair and I quickly changed, in an obvious effort to win the race to the first tee. Time would not permit us to play behind a four ball. We won. Barely pausing to swing a club to loosen stiff muscles, we teed it up and, successfully, hit the fairway on our first tentative swings. We were off. It was another clear but cold morning and Alastair delighted in showing me his course. There was some construction being done to lengthen several holes because it was to be a qualifying course for the 2004 Open to be played the following year at Royal Troon. The Glasgow Golf Club, Gailes Links dates from 1787 and boasts the motto *Semper*

Cum Superbia. The course is a delightful test of one's accuracy, with heather bounding most fairways and the ubiquitous bunkers guarding almost every hole. Alastair and I played quickly and, for the most part efficiently, chatting our way through the chilly morning and delighting in each other's companionship, as golfers from around the world do as members of this fraternity. We finished our round in three hours. Alastair observed that the speed with which we played could have consequences for him in the future. At some distant time when he explained to his wife that the reason he was late was because his round of golf last four and one half hours, Eileen could reply, "Well, you and Jim Coomer played in three hours."

We seemed to be well within Alastair's schedule so, after a quick change of clothes, back into jackets and ties, we sat in the clubhouse for a cup of coffee. When we returned to Copper Beech, Jane and George were chatting in the lounge. Alastair and George were members of the local Rotary Club and were acquainted with each other. After a quick exchange of greetings and good-byes, Alastair left. It had been a delightful morning. I hoped that he was not going to be late for his commitment. We thanked George profusely for his hospitality and promised to return soon.

(I regret to write that since our visit, George has died from a heart attack. He was a delightful and entertaining host. Norma is continuing to operate the Copper Beech as a bed and breakfast.)

I changed into a turtleneck sweater and windbreaker. After packing my golf clubs into their travel bag, I loaded the luggage into our car. It was a few minutes after noon and our scheduled trip had been fulfilled. We now had the rest of the afternoon to relax before driving to our hotel at the airport and returning our hired car. We decided that more coffee was in order over which we would recount to each other our morning activities.

The lounge of the Marine Hotel in Troon faces the eighteenth fairway of the Royal Troon Golf Course. Its walls are lined with pictures of former winners of the Open when played at Royal Troon. We found two comfortable chairs in front of a large window and settled in. Glancing at the menu, it occurred to us that through this entire trip, we had not indulged ourselves with scones, topped with butter, jam, and cream. We immediately set out to remedy that oversight. Coffee, scones, a view out over the fairways of Royal Troon with the Island of Arran outlined on the horizon; it was a wonderful way to enjoy our last afternoon of this wonderful trip. I recounted to Jane my morning's round of golf with Alastair and she told me about her wanderings down the beach to the central area of Troon. Other people came and went but we ordered another pot of coffee and sat contentedly in each other's company reliving some of the past week's memorable moments. We knew that when we left this room, our holiday was, for all intents and purposes, over.

There was one last call to make. We had promised Alastair Symington that we would visit his church before we left town. He had called his secretary and told her to expect us. The Old Parish Church is in the center of Troon. Its exterior is stone and its interior is the dark wood one is accustomed to seeing in these older churches. The high pulpit with its curved wooden staircase, from which Alastair preaches, was particularly impressive to one like me whose life has been one of speaking. I imagined how satisfying it must be to speak from such a pulpit in such a beautiful environment. The secretary gave us a brief history of the stained glass windows through which the afternoon light was being filtered in a mosaic of magical colors. We could understand Alastair's pride (if that's an appropriate word to apply to a minister) at being the pastor of this historic Parish church. We thanked the secretary for the tour and returned to our car. We must now head toward the Glasgow airport.

It isn't so much getting to an airport that is difficult, it is getting around at airports after one arrives. The Holiday Inn Airport Hotel, where I have spent my last night in Glasgow on other occasions, is conveniently located directly across the street from the check-in counters of British Airways. The airport roads getting to it, however, all seemed to be one-way in the opposite direction. When I finally found the parking area of the hotel, I also found a dearth of parking spaces, which did not deter other drivers from parking wherever they could find space. I thought, "Oh, God! After ten days on the road, I am going to scratch up this car in a hotel parking lot thirty minutes before returning it." I found a little space clearly marked "No Parking" and parked. Jane and I rolled our bags into the lobby to check in. I now had another problem: I hadn't a clue as to how to get to the car hire agency. I walked over to the airport to use the direct line to the agency. I asked if they had a van coming to the airport that I could follow back to the agency. I was told no, but was given directions. Great! With Jane as navigator, we tried to extract ourselves from the airport. This took almost as long as it had taken to drive from Troon to Glasgow. Finally I saw a sign with a name I recognized as being one given to me in my directions. We took a chance. Several miles later, another familiar name appeared. So far, so good. Making one last turn Jane said, "Let's try this road." We did and, to my left, fortunately, we found the very spot from which we had set forth over a week earlier. Our relief was palpable. As the young man behind the counter checked our paperwork, I mentioned the flat tire. Since I had punctured the sidewall, I knew that I was going to have to replace the tire. It was to cost me an additional $100 dollars. Even at that price, it was less expensive than AA was going to charge just to change the tire. Jane and I thanked the agency personnel for their services and climbed into a van to be returned to the airport hotel. Our driver was the young man who had checked our car over when we returned it. He assured us that we were neither the first, nor would we be the last, to have punctured a tire. On the way to the airport he regaled us with stories of damaged hired cars returned by tourists. By the time we got to the hotel, we were convinced that we were among the best tourist drivers ever to hire a car from this agency.

With no lingering entanglements, we now had little to do but wait. We wandered into the hotel dining room to check the menu. We wanted something light. The hostess recommended the bar. We each ordered a beer and checked the bar menu. Their offerings were too light, mainly bar snacks. We finished our beers and walked across the street to the airport. After wandering through several eating areas and not being able to agree on what it was we wanted to eat, we saw a familiar sign: Burger King. There were no longer doubts.

The pace of the week, aided by the beer, caught up with us and we fell asleep watching the BBC news. Having stuffed every day to its fullest for over a week and with no agenda on the morrow except to be on time for our flights, we fell asleep quickly and slept soundly. The day, the week, and the trip ended in a restful and a peaceful sleep.

Day Eleven

Jane and I knew that today would be a long day of travel and sitting. Food and drink would be plentiful but walking about to burn off calories would be limited. We nibbled at a light breakfast in the hotel, since breakfast was included in the cost of our room. One of the perks in staying at this particular hotel is that arriving passengers at the airport across the street push their baggage trolleys to the hotel and then leave them there for departing passengers to return to the airport with their baggage. Although our route to Glasgow had been through Manchester, our route home was via British Airways to London's Gatwick airport and then a Delta flight to Atlanta. Our BA flight left Glasgow at 9:25am. At 8:00am we were at the British Airway check-in counter checking three bags straight through to Atlanta. I would continue to lug our twenty-pound carry-on bag for another day.

The flight from Glasgow to London is only about one hour. We would then have a two hour wait before we could board our Delta flight for the last leg of our journey home. London's Gatwick airport is familiar territory for Jane and me. When we lived in Houston, Texas, our flights to England flew into Gatwick. In the past, we had spent a number of hours wandering about the international concourse at this airport, shopping in the multitude of shops and duty free shops and, generally observing the international scene. On this stop, however, we headed for Delta's Crown Room to relax in some comfortable chairs, drink some coffee, and read the morning newspapers. Our flight was called on schedule, became airborne within five minutes of its stated departure time, and Jane and I settled in for a nine hour flight home. One is always pleased when flights are uneventful. With some light food, light drinks, some reading, and a nap the time passed with minimum discomfort or boredom. At a little before 5:00pm, we were beginning our approach into Atlanta. We landed a few minutes ahead of schedule.

The fact that Jane and I were seated in the front of the airplane allowed us to be nearly the first passengers in line at U.S. Customs. We presented our passports and our list of purchases to the Customs agent. After the customary questions and the stamping of our passports, he said those words that are always music to me when returning from a trip abroad:

"Welcome home."

I don't know if Custom agents are required to say those words but, for me, I look forward to hearing them. It is as though it is an official welcome home. Thank you U.S. Customs Service.

Returning to Atlanta from any international destination requires one to pick up one's luggage, go through the Customs inspection then, replace one's luggage on a conveyer belt to be taken to the baggage claim in the main terminal. It is a cumbersome, but necessary requirement due to the physical structure of the Atlanta airport. This also requires queuing up for another security check since, presumably, someone could extract a weapon of some sort from their checked luggage and hold the airport hostage. Free at last, we caught the underground train to the main terminal and retrieved our baggage. Our daughter was waiting and although our body time read 1:00am, we were delighted to relive our trip in response to her many questions during the drive home.

Home is such a wonderful word. One drives up to a house, opens a door and, suddenly, it becomes a home. We will unpack tomorrow. *Our* bed is waiting. Tomorrow, upon reflection, I think we may conclude that this was (possibly) the best (golf) vacation ever.